Already Rich

SECRETS TO MASTER YOUR MONEY MIND

Reveal Your Magnetic Wealth Vibe
Be *Irresistible* to Money

By Nan Akasha, CHT

What people are saying about "Already Rich"

"I have known Nan for years and thoroughly enjoyed reading "Already Rich; Secrets to Master Your Money Mind". Nan's heart and sincere desire to reveal the true path to riches jumps off each page. Rich with affirmations, full of profound insights and practical strategies, this book is a gem. I highly recommend it!"
- Dr. Joe Vitale   Author
"Attract Money Now" and "Zero Limits"

"Nan's 'Already Rich' book is the exact thing that people need to read right now who are struggling and stressed out about money. It's more than just powerful affirmations this book really allows you to identify what your money blocks are while giving you the tools you can use to shift your money vibe instantly into attraction mode."

- Heather Picken
"The Spirit Trainer"
Best selling author, Spiritual Life Coach,
Hypnotherapist, and founder of the Quantum
Entrepreneur Program.
www.TheSpiritTrainer.com

"Nan Akasha's new book, 'Already Rich': will transform your relationship with money. You'll find affirmations that will touch you at a deep level, and each section reveals hidden principles of wealth. The book also offers stories of Nan's own journey to prosperity and freedom. Above

all, each page radiates the enthusiasm, positive energy, and love that has already attracted so many to Nan Akasha's work."

- Jillian Coleman Wheeler
GrantMeRich.com

"As the founder of AbundanceUnlimited.com. I get a lot of books across my desk asking for an endorsement. Nan Akasha's 'Already Rich' is a book I highly endorse. I received the very first copy and dove right into it. It is exactly what people need in the current economic climate. Nothing is more important than your mindset and your money mindset influences so much of your life. This book is what's needed by people that are struggling and stressed out about money. It has more than powerful affirmations (which it has tons of), Nan's Manifesting Formula and meditation alone will help to identify your money blocks and gives you the tools to shift your money vibrations."

- Christopher Sherrod
Author of "PlayProsperityGames.com"
AbundanceUnlimited.com

"Nan Akasha's 'Already Rich' will expand your consciousness around how you can tap into the great riches that surround us and await u s all. If you are not abundant or living in extreme opulence where money is no object, you likely have some deep seated issues around money. Are you doing endless good with the knowledge that there is an unending supply of wealth ready for each of us to tap into? No? Then get Nan's book"

- Dr. Joe Rubino   Founder of
CenterForPersonalReinvention.com, Author,
TheSelfEsteemBook.com

"Already Rich is a hypnotic, transformational experience in the disguise of a book. It transforms you on a cellular level as you read each page, which is sprinkled with powerful affirmations. I can literally feel the energy bursting from each paragraph and into my psyche. Great job, Nan!"

- Rhonda Ryder
Founder of KidsAwakening.com

"The more I read your book, the more I realized it wasn't a simple motivational tool and that you have the depth behind your work that can motivate people. My thought is that your experiences make it very real and reachable for people who feel like they have a 'missing link' when it comes to generating personal wealth. I thoroughly enjoyed having you on my 'Spirit & Energy' tele seminar series. Thank you for being present for our listeners. You were right with me! For that I am so grateful, thank you."

- Nina Wallinder
layersofhealth.com

What people are saying about Nan Akasha

"Nan has these huge spiritual wings of light. She asks the most deep, interesting questions."

- Joe Vitale
star of "The Secret" and
author of "The Attractor Factor"

"I was just listening to your interview, my o my you are goooood! I love the way you put it over, you know your stuff, we must have you on (our radio show) again! Nan has a way of condensing law of attraction and metaphysical concepts into an easy to understand and fun way, I thoroughly recommend anything she does!"

- Neil Long
England Host and CO Creator with Terah Nina Ferrel of
'The Conscious Creation Radio Show'
consciouscreationshow.com

"Nan has the heart of a lion, if I was lost at sea, I would want her with me. People want to hear what she has to say..."''

- Dr. Ihaleakala Hew Len
Co-Author of Zero Limits with Dr. Joe Vitale and
Ho'oponopono Specialist

"The reason I am so excited about Nan's work is that since I began working with her Money Muse program, I have had $3500 of unexpected income, bonuses and freebies since December 1. Pretty impressive."
Nan Akasha is the fairy Godmother of Money. I have changed my whole relationship with money and feel so connected.

I feel a whole new world has opened up to me...thanks!"
- Catherine Behan
San Diego, CA
soulmatesavvy.com

"Nan is a terrific women I met at workshops with my friend and co-author, Joe Vitale. Like Joe and like me, she believes strongly in the Law of Attraction, and is a talented guide for anyone who wants to learn how to manifest wealth."
- Jillian Wheeler
co author "Your Internet Cash Machine" with Joe Vitale

"Thank you so much... I learned soooo much!! I believe it has changed by life. I must share with you some results I've experienced since beginning the class. I am a real estate investor and I sell my homes on a Lease Purchase Basis. I had been really struggling with my business, but since beginning the class I filled 2 of my properties with great tenant buyers, sold a property for a profit of 35K and getting ready to close on another sale for a profit for of 25K. I'd say the spirit is flowing!! Thank you... sooo much!!"
- Michele Ashton Dysert

"Nan is such a natural and practical communicator. She embodies not only the Spirit of Money but is an energetic generator of joy, freedom and abundance. As a person, Nan is passionately living an expansive life of inspired action, where she naturally and practically demonstrates all the fun and happiness that is our earthly heritage. Nan is a being of great light and vivacity, who epitomizes the notion of self - determination and in aligning with her

true nature inspires all of us to reach our full potential and be unlimited potentiality itself."

- Natasha Hewitt
Manchester U.K.

"Nan was awesome at getting to the core of what I could not see for myself on multiple occasions because I was to close to the subject. First, and most importantly, she managed to help me release a block I have had for 36 years and was associated with an insurance settlement I received from my mom dying in a car accident. I had an unrecognized block that acquiring money without having to work hard for it equaled death. This scenario was intensified when I received money from an uncle dying and then receiving money from my grandmother dying.

Since I received the coaching from Nan I have been able to accept money in my life and for it to come in an easy and relaxed manner in a healthy and positive way. I also have been able to cut my hours in half and still have the income I desire to live a satisfying life with multiple vacations every year.

She is more than generous with her time and talents having multiple free calls every month so you can get a feel for her style. I can highly recommend you being on them and hiring her for one on one coaching no matter what you may be needing help with. Nan has a heart of gold and she has made me feel like I am a worthy addition to the human race."

Year first hired: 2008 (hired more than once).

Top Qualities: Great Results, Good Value, Creative.

- Sylvia Svihel

"My Dear Nan: My sincere thanks and deep appreciation for what you have given to me. I really do admire you

sooo much for the inspiration, the motivation, your words of wisdom, your words of encouragement, the love you share, you are truly an amazing and unique woman and I love you for that!

When I listen to you I am so amazed at you and think, I would love to be like you and share that kind of inspiration and spirituality with people who seems lost with no hope. May be one day, I will! Once again a hearth felt thank you for being you. Nan, I embrace your world with enormous gratitude and with everything you said in your email I am looking forward to living my dreams and the life I deserve from being successful in my online Internet business. Take care and God Bless!

- Sandra W.

"I am still marveling at our session together, and the Everything has a voice class...huge impacts in my life with my husband, myself, my thoughts...keep up the life changing work :) Blessings, Tami"

- Tami Gulland,
TamiGulland.com, Madison, WI

"OMG OMG OMG OMG U R Not GOING TO BELIEVE THIS!!! Nan, Nan, Nan, Nan, Nan, Nan, NAN!!! !!! !!!
I AM TOTALLY BLOWN AWAY!!! During the class, a friend called and "had to speak to me right away" Long story short she came and gave me $260.00!!! She just had the feeling that I needed it right now!!! BUT the most amazing part is When you were mentioning the products, I said "Oh please God, let me be able to purchase the Spirit of Money somehow" It would be so awesome if that happened ASAP. WHAM!!! WHO KNEW IT WAS GOING TO BE THIS EASY!!! WOW!!! WOW!!! WOW!!! WOW!!! WOW!!! WOW!!!

Dear Lady, OH WOW!!! OH WOW!!! OH WOW!!! OH WOW!!! I am almost speechless. I don't think I am going to sleep much tonight!!! I LOVE YOU!!! AWESOME LADY!!! THANK YOU THANK YOU THANK YOU THANK YOU THANK YOU THANK YOU!!!"

- Val

"Hi Nan, Some Really Big changes for all WOO HOO! and YEAH!I too, got some money during the class. Really neat.This is all really cool stuff. Thank you, thank you, thank you. Blessings, Sandy"

- Sandy

"Hi Nan, I'm up at 2:00 am checking emails! Just wanted to drop you a note and tell you how much I enjoy and benefit from the Intend Global Healing calls. Your voice is so soothing, and I can feel the sincerity of your meditations. I pray you never run out of subjects or inspiration for these calls."

- Jim Brown

"Nan, I also wanted to thank you for your openness and high-value sharing from your warm heart. Just hearing how your life is being guided adds confidence to my being that I am aligning with the Flow. I resonate so wonderfully with your energy that I feel as if we could be sisters. Of course, we are. Much Love, Namaste, Kristine Johnson"

"Hi Nan- I wanted to let you know how talented you are. What a fantastic class you put on last night. I wrote down pages and pages of new information for me which I want to remember and use. You have a great ability to

communicate. I will study and listen to all of your tapes. Thank you for all of your great work. Your Friend, Marty"

- Marty Rowland
Winchester, MA IMS-online.com/Boston

"Hi Nan, I want to say a BIG Thank You for our inspirational conversation today. I loved what you said and you inspired me and gave me so many new ways to think about how to approach my life, book and wealth creation. What a wonderful connection and I am so very grateful to you for your work, your inspiring calls and talking with you a little while ago has given me so much inspiration and more confidence to go forward anew with renewed enthusiasm. I feel "on the road" again and I am so genuinely grateful to you. Many, many thanks again and also I was delighted to hear about your speaking on a LOA cruise. Good going! You deserve the best. Warmly, Margie"

- Margie

"THANK YOU THANK YOU THANK YOU!I AM STANDING HERE, WITH OPEN ARMS AND HEART!!!! SOOOO GRATEFUL FOR ALL YOUR WONDERFUL INSPIRATION…. The way you woke us up to our limiting thoughts with such humor and love was amazing! We're truly grateful. Have a wonderful evening. Such love, Kate and Philip, Australia"

- Kate and Philip
Australia

"Dear Nan, Thank you so much for the special message, I liked it so much I forwarded it on to my friends. I love to listen in on your Global Healing telecast. I am increasing the word about you. I love your program for a number of reasons, you basically are the only one that speaks and you do that for quite a long time. I feel like you are sitting across from me just shooting the breeze and you are easy to follow.

Thank you for being there and for your enormous generosity of time, information and spirit.
I wish all the beautiful things you sent to me to go back to you... Love, Sheila :)"

- Sheila

Dedication

I dedicate this book to the field of abundance, also referred to as The Universe (Source, Divine, God/Goddess). All gifts, love, joy and wealth flow endlessly from here, from within us, as we are the Divine wellspring of abundance. I am deeply grateful.

I dedicate this book to my beautiful, brilliant, fun, intelligent twin daughters, Emily and Sierra. You are my true riches. You make my heart sing and are the treasure of my life. You bless me with being you, being authentic. You are already infinitely wealthy in all ways. I am impressed daily with your wit and humor. I love sharing life with you. You grasped the secret of attraction before age 5 and are amazing manifesters. I love the adventure of life we are traveling together. I love you with all my being, now, and always.

I dedicate this book to my beloved, my soul mate, the love of my life, Chris. You enrich every moment. Your love is so full, rich, deep, true, allowing, supportive and inspiring. You are the most amazing man I have ever encountered. Your deep patience, endless appreciation, pure, vast, gentle heart amaze me daily. You hold a space for me that allows me to be me, and for me to soar. With you, all things are possible. You are right my love, "Above all is love". My deepest gratitude and unending love are yours. Thanks for creating a fun, rich life with me! "Everything's going so well!"

Already Rich

SECRETS TO MASTER YOUR MONEY MIND

Reveal Your
Magnetic Wealth Vibe
Be *Irresistible* to Money

By Nan Akasha, CHT

My Mission

To transform the world through Wealth Consciousness.

A wealthy world full of empowered, joyful people with a Wealth Mindset, who know how to tune their Wealth Vibe to their true inner purpose and live in Authentic Wealth. Wealth is happiness.

Rich blessings, Nan

"The key is not the mere pursuit of wealth, but changing your beliefs and attitudes about it."

- ANTHONY ROBBINS

ACKNOWLEDGMENTS

I simply want to share this:

Over the last 22+ years I have traveled a varied and wondrous path. I have read, studied, experienced, learned and absorbed many paths. I send love and great appreciation to every philosophy, healing technique, Shaman, yoga, meditation teacher, seminar leader, and guide who has shared their light and perspective with me.

The books, courses, certifications workshops... All have added to who I AM, and how I see and experience the world. I love to learn, discover, and dive into new adventures, and have loved traveling the world experiencing phenomenal enlightening moments with many beautiful beings. There are too many of you to mention and my heart knows and honors you all.

I would like to mention a few special beings who were catalysts for opening new doors within me:

Alton Kamadon

Benu & Karen

WHAT I GIVE TO YOU

When you enter my world, this is what I give to you, always, and all ways.

I see increase in wealth, health, happiness and love.

I request for self expression, self esteem and self worth to flow from within you in an endless flow.

I accept Abundance in all you desire.

I claim courage, strength, compassion for you.

I know you now allow yourself to align with the BEST in all.

I believe in you.

I invite you to, and hold a space for you to open your heart and let your light and beauty shine.

I Thank You for Being YOU, for adding to the creation of a world of infinite delight and wealth.

I Honor you for choosing to BE here now and for Being in my world.

Welcome to my reality; one of limitless joy, love, riches, health, happiness, friends, creating, uplifting, inspiration and expansion.

Live Your Dream! It is here NOW.

~ Nan Akasha

"Lack of money is the root of all evil."

- George Bernard Shaw

"FREE YOUR MIND AND THE WEALTH WILL FOLLOW."

- NAN AKASHA

"I AM ALREADY RICH, I FEEL RICH, I KNOW I AM RICH, I CAN SEE MYSELF AS RICH."

- NAN AKASHA

NAN INVITES YOU TO FREE YOUR MIND

INTRODUCTION

"You'll discover how every alteration in your thoughts affects your awareness, the energy all around. Change your thoughts, change your world. This is not about using your mind to change behaviors. It is much easier.
It is about using your mind to change your energy so that the behavior automatically changes. The same holds true for every area of your life."
— Jeddah Mali

Imagine a sea, a beautiful blue ocean, and it is the vibration of wealth... you are floating in it, buoyed up by it. There are wealth vibes as far as you can see in every direction. As you float in this sea of vibration, safe and happy, the sun shining on your face, you feel deep inner peace and joy... you know you are supported and held by this massive sea of wealth energy. As far as you can see in any direction the blue ocean of wealth extends, there is no end to it.

This is literally reality. You exist within, and are permeated by, the field of Abundance..... an unending sea of energy, ready and waiting to BE whatever you desire! You have access to a limitless supply of raw material to create whatever you want, including all the wealth you desire! Really! So, this is not hype, happy thinking and 'let's all hold hands and hope we get rich" stuff... this is fact, science and reality!

Do you feel you are able to manifest wealth when you desire it? Do you feel at ease with money, income and cash flow? Do you trust within you that you are always provided for?

or

Do your dreams feel far away and seemingly impossible to achieve? Do you feel like your life has passed you by and you may never have the wealth that will make your dreams possible?

So many people I talk to, coach and teach feel lost, sad, and full of regrets. Feel like their dreams have faded to dust because they can never seem to get money to come to them in a consistent and abundant way. Many people today feel lost and scared, unsure of their future and in fear of not having enough income to survive. Most of all I find people feel confused, frustrated and even angry. Where is the money? Why won't it come to them? Many wonder what is blocking me? What do I do to prosper?

Well hang on to your hat, that is all about to change!

Are you ready to open the door to your wealth?

I know when we free our minds, we feel clarity, focus, happiness and joy. We are in control of our minds and thoughts and we choose what we want to think, see, and feel. This is true freedom, freedom from within! So, when your mind is free, you can see all the opportunities, joy, love, fun... available to you. When you can see that life is full of well being and possibilities, you naturally feel good and live in the flow. Then you allow the Universe to show you just what to pay attention to, lighting up your way towards what you now desire. It is a fun game, life, when you free your mind and follow the clues, knowing they are there and looking for them! Then life unfolds in such a miraculous way.

Wealthy to me, is abundance in all things you desire, in all areas of life. Wealth has several definitions, one is "an abundance or profusion of anything; plentiful amount: a wealth of imagery." So wealth, in my personal definition is: An abundance of love, joy, health, friends, fun, adventure, travel, spiritual expansion, enlightenment, significance, fulfillment and money flowing easily to and through me, now!

If you're like nearly everyone in the world, you have challenges, emotions and fears around Money. You've been battling your poverty consciousness and limiting wealth beliefs for YEARS. Maybe you don't know why you feel stuck and are not sure what is blocking you. But have you ever stopped to ask yourself why?

I mean really, if you're a divine being from Source, blessed and loved by true Unconditional love and you're capable of limitless possibility, why is it so dang hard to get your finances under control?

Here's what I have discovered:

You are meant to BE Wealthy... in fact by NOT Being Wealthy, you are not aligned with your true purpose and living your full potential! Your "job" is to BE your true Authentic Wealthy self. To explore the world and discover what you love and to share your unique talents with others... and prosper.

If you have felt stuck and not able to take your life in the direction you desire, good news!! This feeling of discomfort with where you are now, your DESIRE for more wealth, all this means; You are ready to transform now! Desire is the evidence that Source, Divine Energy (God) is ASKING to express itself through you! You do desire wealth, you naturally want wealth... this is the way it is meant to be! You want it, because it is your natural state, and you want to re-align with it.

Now you can learn to use your built in systems to create more inner peace, confidence, focus, clarity, joy, and success. Wealth is your natural state.

Also I know that EVERYTHING IS OPPORTUNITY. Bar none. That means every single event, person, situation, whether you see it as good or bad, IS an opportunity for you. You would not have it in your life if it was not the right time for you. It means you are ready, you can handle it and to let go and move forward with faith. Adapt that mindset, and your life changes immediately.

Are you attuned to your personal Purpose?

We need to be clear on our purpose, both our personal big "WHY" and our every day purpose. Your "why" is why are you doing what you are doing? What do you want what you think you want? Why are you willing to do whatever is necessary to achieve your goals? This gives you the direction and the passion to get through anything.

Once you firmly know your why, you will find it much easier to stay focused. I also find that if you cultivate and underlying intention that your purpose in every moment, no matter what you are doing is "to be rich, happy and healthy" (that is mine), you will find doors to wealth open in the most magical places. When you install this as a dominant intent at all times, then you are magnetic to just the right people, resources and events to lead you to being healthy happy and rich! Let the energies work under the surface while you go about your day!

"The simple truth is, if you never choose to be wealthy, you will never attain wealth."
- Richard Paul Evans

You've probably wondered why you're here? What's your purpose? Were you made for something grander? Why aren't you wealthy... you are a good, hardworking person, right?

Guess what... none of that matters!! Yes, it's shocking, but true! Your dreams are not impossible or too risky to pursue. Your wealth does not depend on you obeying anyone's rules, or working hard for 30 years. Your wealth is yours, no matter what, you just have to know how to access it! Your Soul has the design for your life, unveil it!

You can create a win-win with yourself. You don't have to manipulate, overcome, overpower, or otherwise muscle anyone, including yourself to get what you want. You only have to understand how you work, how the Universe and energy works, and how to align these systems. Live the life your Soul intended, it's rich!

And you can follow your bliss -- listen to your Highest Self -- but you WON'T have to go broke, start over, take a long time, be exhausted, go back to school, follow a lot of rules, or anything else you THINK you have to do to live your Wealthy, passionate life.

Now is the time.

Now is the only time, ever. If you do not learn this now, what will happen tomorrow, next month, next year? What if you keep on the same path, nothing changes... will you be OK with that? Most likely you have experienced things not changing month after month, sometimes year after year. Choose now to transform!

Are you ready to feel good? Are you ready to release the doubt and fear and step into a new phase of life? Here is your opportunity. Take it. You have asked and asked, right? You have dreamed and wished and hoped. Here is your answer... empower yourself now and begin to live your dream.

All you have to lose is the pain and struggle of the past ... and that's a good thing! I know you can make your life happen, but only you can decide. Only you can act. Only you can say "Yes, now is my time and I am taking the reigns to my life!"

Invest in yourself, your life, your family and your happiness! This is a doorway to being a conscious manifester. I encourage you to find the courage and commitment within you now. There is no time like now, literally.

In order to receive the Money you have wanted, you must ask, take action and claim it. In order to have what you want you must know how to communicate your vision. In order to do what you most desire, you must trust that desire within you... it is the power to succeed. Now come find out how!

Imagine in just one month, feeling ease and abundance with Money, in a way you never knew before...

You must choose... no one else can do it for you!

Follow these concepts and use these affirmations or statements of limitless potential. Commit to 30 days or more of using these, every day, and watch your life transform!

Here's a tip on aligning with money

Money is just like a person. Money is energy. Money is attracted to energy that loves it, and appreciates it. When you realize you have a *relationship* with money, it all changes and you begin to be aware of your attitude (usually negative) towards money.

The Voice of Money says:

"I am attracted to those who love me, appreciate me, and respect me.

I love to seek out those who have fun with me, play with me, enjoy me...

I am magnetically drawn to those who find joy and inspiration with me, get excited to see me, expect me to come...

it is most fun to play with those who play full out, who think of possibilities and

anticipate great things when I show up."

"MONEY LOVES ME, MONEY RUNS TO ME, PLAYS WITH ME, STAYS WITH ME."

- NAN AKASHA

PURPOSE OF THIS BOOK

"Out of nothing and out of no way,
a way will be made."
- Michael Beckwith

I believe we all create our reality. My main website is called www.createyourownrealitynow.com. I have realized, in over 23 years of self discovery, that the only way to create true change is to take 100% responsibility for myself. That means the way I feel, think, act, react, speak. That means I choose what I decide to do, what I make things mean and if I allow others to influence me. I spent most of my life as a people pleaser. Seeking my validation, worth and approval from outside of me. That is a no win battle for sure. You must come to the point where you realize this is your life. You are the only one who can live it, experience it, choose it, and create it. You might as well decide to do that now, and let go of what everyone else thinks. When you decide to love yourself, accept yourself, approve of yourself and ask for what you want, life become magical.

I want to share what I have discovered so you and all of us can begin to live authentic lives, with authentic wealth, that flows in a never ending supply. The field of abundance is always ready to give us all the wealth, joy, love, health and happiness we *decide to allow ourselves to have.* In my years of searching, learning, teaching and traveling, I have come to this philosophy:

- Life is meant to be fun.
- Life is designed to be full, rich, abundant and wealthy.
- Life is satisfying, challenging, exciting... an adventure.
- Now is the only moment to embrace our vision of what we truly want, from deep within us.
- Now is the time to see it, ask for it, accept it, and claim it.
- Be the master of your reality. Create your life on purpose. Now now now.
- Our mind is a powerful ally. It frames our life experience and solves all problems for us by making us aware of opportunities that will lead us to that which we want. We just have to be aware and cultivate the courage to take the opportunities as they come.
- Honor, trust and love yourself, you are the only one who can choose, and enjoy your life. Live for yourself and you will have more to give others!

My intention is to discover the fastest, easiest and most fun way to create what we want. What goes to the core and gets results. Easy and fun and let's enjoy life. Sound good?

So here I share my philosophy, my inspiration, my tools, and my passion. I share how to use your mind, energy and self image to create the wealth, riches, money, cash flow, income, and joy you desire.

I love meditation and active visualization. I love creating a wealthy mindset and using my mind to create the experience of wealth I love. Our mind is the gateway to our reality. We can create new habits, and neural pathways that make us magnetic to wealth. These make it easy, automatic and natural to feel, think and act as if you are already rich.

"I am already rich, I feel rich, I know I am rich, I can see myself as rich."

This book is a manual for manifestation. It can guide you to intentionally living and creating the life that your Soul intended, which means flow, ease, joy, inspiration, wealth. It will show you what works and how to work together with your mind, and your energy systems... how you work. It will show you how to really use affirmations or "Statements of limitless Potential", (SLP's) to supercharge your beliefs and speed of manifesting. It is also designed to take you deeper into your understanding of how your mind, energy and vision work together in perfect harmony to literally create that which you claim as yours.

You are magnetic, and you can increase your magnetism, to money, people, anything. Throughout the book there are 'magnetic processes' for you. I recommend getting a journal just for your journey through this book. You can write the affirmations you want to use, use the processes, create your new wealth image and more.

Using affirmations

Using affirmations, or what I prefer to call "Statements of limitless Potential", is more than saying some words, more than repeating them over and over and more than thinking positive.

All these things have merit and have a place. However affirmations, the way most people use them, are the slow road to paradise! Because of the way your mind works, you would need a long time to create real transformation that creates results in your life experience. Perhaps you know what I am talking about. Have you been using affirmations and positive thinking for awhile with occasional and weak results? Most people have.

Our reality, so to speak, is simply how we are experiencing our lives. It is how we interpret, frame and react to events. The great news is, we have total control over how we experience life. We are the only ones experiencing our lives, after all. We can choose what we make things mean and how we act. When we understand that we are in the 'captain's chair' of our life and if we aren't steering and planning where we want to go on purpose, we are wandering through life. This does not give us happiness, wealth, love and a feeling of accomplishment, significance. It is creating by default, and it also gives you the feeling of having no control of your life. This is powerlessness. It's time to choose to use your power.

The main keys to creating a wealthy life, and tuning in to the reality that you are 'already rich', are:

- your mind.
- your energy.

Learn to manage your energy, focus it where you want it. Do not waste it on the past or the pain. This way you will find power to create unlike anything you have experienced.

Secret Keys to Master Your Money Mind

Learn to master your mind, especially your money mind, and you can have the life you dream of.

When you can think, what you want to think, what you want to be true for you, despite what your life looks like around you, no matter what is going on, you can think the truth.

When you can hold one thought for a minute, you move mountains. This is why I say "free your mind and the wealth will follow".

This book is to *free your mind*. From what you have been thinking that has not brought you what you really want. From thinking about what you don't want. From repeating unserving, unsupportive thoughts. From doubt, fear and unbelief in your power and your worthiness.

The book "Think and Grow Rich" by Napoleon Hill is not 'worry and grow rich", it's not "work hard and suffer and grow rich" and it's not "wait for someone else to do it for you or blame someone else and grow rich". It is THINK... and you will grow rich. Simple, powerful, true.

So all I ask is you suspend your disbelief. Take this journey into your true self with me and let go of the doubts and "what if's"... what do you have to lose? Poverty consciousness, worry and anger towards money? Good, let it go and open your mind. Tune in to your energy.

Let's change your relationship with money and activate your WEALTH VIBE. Let's get magnetic to wealth and worthiness!

Oh, and one more thing. Time to love yourself, allow yourself, believe in yourself and value yourself. You are unique, beautiful, talented, powerful, wealthy, interesting, valued and here for a reason. You are the only one who can live your life. Decide to live it now.

Let's go.

"I Am the Master of My Money Mind."

- Nan Akasha

STEP INTO YOUR MASTERY

Chapter 1

"If you are not willing to risk the unusual, you will have to settle for the ordinary..."
- Jim Rohn

Choose Your Life! You can HAVE, BE and DO anything!

Welcome! I am honored you are here. My intent is to inspire you to truly KNOW, deep inside of you, that you do Create Your Own Reality ...and you can do it intentionally...NOW! I am inspired by life and love and joy and I want to touch, move and empower you to feel the same.

You already created everything in your life...and even if you do not have the life you truly want, YET, it is GOOD news!

It is proof that you are a powerful creator!

You have attracted the people, situations and literally everything, consciously or unconsciously. Now that you know how powerful you are at manifesting, you can begin to use these ideas to intentionally create whatever you want, in every area of your life. All creation is communication. When we clearly communicate to our minds, the field of abundance, and others, we align with what we want and get it. Learning how to communicate what we desire is the key to getting it and living it. Each system, within and without communicates in its own special way.

The Universe does not say 'No'

*A caution; I often hear people say how easily they give up on what they want, thinking it is a sign from the Divine. I beg to differ. In fact, in my experience if you do not commit to what you want, if you do not persist, keep looking for a solution and hold to the vision of what you want, you may never get it. I hear things like "well I called you and the phone call didn't go through, so I figured I wasn't meant to talk to you", or some version of this. Does the Universe send you messages? Yes. However, it is almost an epidemic how many people just fall into complacency and think they are not meant to have what they want when something does not work the first time. Don't give up so easily! Do not look to interpret signs and events as 'you are not meant to have this' before you persist. "Well, I really, really wanted to go to this event, but the sign up did not work, so I guess I am not meant to..." These are disempowering, false interpretations. If you are willing to give up what you truly desire so easily, and let anything appear as an excuse, you will see little in your life that you really love. People who succeed and have what they want, did not take no, did not give up, they kept looking for the right path.

The Universe does not say no, and does not think you do not deserve. There may, however, be a better path, an easier, route or you may need to strengthen some skills, desire or focus, and that is what the signs mean. Choose to see the signs as a way of guiding, and then allow the real message to reveal itself as you move forward.

We actually have to be masters of our focus and persist, daily, in focusing on what we want and keep the signal strong and consistent. We are training ourselves, our minds as well as communicating to the energy, the Divine mind, the Universal intelligence. *It is this absolute decisiveness and faith that produces the miracles of manifestation.* Don't give up your dream. Read the signs, persist and keep moving forward.

How to Communicate

When we understand how to communicate our desires, we receive them. For our purposes here, we need to know these forms of communication and when to use them. After all, affirmations or Statements of limitless potential (SLP's) are one way of communicating, in the hopes of attracting wealth and achieving that which we are affirming.

- Our Mind communicates in pictures; visualize.
- Our body communicates in feelings, be silent and feel.
- Our inner being communicates in intuition through emotion/passion/desire.
- Our Heart communicates in love , vibrations and is a powerful magnet, therefore is our attraction center.

- The Universe, God, the field of abundance communicates through gratitude.

How to you use your energy systems with affirmations

Affirmations are a way to focus energy in on something specific you desire. In order to effectively communicate this, we need to understand our systems. We are energetic beings, with many energy systems that work together with the Universe and the field of abundance to create whatever we decide we want. Our main systems are:

1. Our Mind.
2. Our Emotions.
3. Our Heart.
4. Our Energy.
5. The Field of Abundance.

These are all energetic systems you have within and around you. They work for you, never against you. You simply need to understand how they work and reprogram what you have chosen to believe. What you believe is true for you. When you get all of your energy moving in the same direction, you flow and create. There will always be situations that challenge you and they are all opportunities. Like a workout, you get stronger, more confident and more at peace.

"I am a powerful creator. I accept my Divine creative abilities and allow them to guide my life."

It is to your advantage to accept that these systems work together for your highest good. Allow them to help you, stop thinking you have to make it all happen on your own. You are not alone.

Manifest

1. *Ask, expect, claim it.*
2. Allow your mind to picture what you want.
3. Let your emotions add passion fuel.
4. Build the sensations and the energy around what you want, seeing it always as done, existing right now.
5. Allow the field of abundance to work with you.
6. Combine the vision, the passion and then move it into your heart with gratitude and love. Then let your heart release the energized vision out into the field of abundance.
7. Use your affirmations or statements of limitless potential to help you see the vision, and feel what it will feel like when it is true for you in 3-D.

Appreciate what you have AND what you are expecting

Gratitude. Gratitude has power deeper then you can imagine. It is how you keep a clear communication open to the Universe, the field of abundance, Divine. It is gratitude must be a part of your energy, consciously and un. Appreciating what you have now, people and things in your life, is all very important. We must always start where we are now. Accept it and appreciate it, it is your jumping off point. Also, the more you practice gratitude towards what is, the more you will see and receive to appreciate. (see my blogs on "looking for what you want").

There is another level of gratitude too. In manifesting, creating, attracting, the more powerful level of gratitude, is in then appreciating what you want as if it were *already here*. Remember all possibilities exist right now. You ARE already rich. So to truly tune in to the riches that are there for you, you must first appreciate them, as if they were already visible, useable and tangible in all ways. This creates trust and expectancy. This adds to your magnetic vibe.

Be grateful for the wealth you desire, yet is not manifest yet!

You can have anything, whether anyone else thinks so or not. Getting yourself into a genuine place of gratitude, where you know what you want, you feel you deserve it, you are excited about getting it and you have no doubts or guilt about it at all will accelerate your manifestation!

Be grateful for what you have...AND what you want and know is on its way to you. You do not have to settle for less than what you want in any area of your life! You can have it all. Do you believe that? Build up your belief and create your life now!!! Gratitude attracts more of what you are grateful for!

See in joy. Feel rich now, until it appears all around you!

Magnetic Process:

Why I have seen the movie "The Secret" over 50 times

I hope you have seen the amazing, uplifting and inspiring movie "The Secret". It is all about Creating your own reality, now! I have seen it so many times I have lost track! Literally! I have seen it well over 50 times. I watched it alone, with my kids and with friends. I put it on as background, like music when I was putzing around the house. I love it.

The "The Secret" is The Law of Attraction...like attracts like. You sow what you reap....you get back what you give out....people treat you like you treat them. You create your reality with the power of your thoughts and your feelings.

"I choose what I put into my mind. I repeat only empowering, positive and possibility filled thoughts."

The reason I have watched it so many times is, I know how the mind works. Repetition. I have also experienced the power of the Law of Attraction in my life so many times, knowingly and unknowingly, intentionally and unintentionally. It is powerful, it is real and it is there for you to use to create what you want. Once I understood the way it worked, I was empowered to ask for what I wanted and know how to make it manifest. It takes practice and action, but it works, every time, for everyone.

I also repeat watching the movie 'The Secret" because as a master level hypnotist I know the power of programming your mind by repeating things. The more you repeat, the more it goes into your subconscious mind as true for you. (This is why it is important to be careful watching TV, I never watch the news). If there is something you want to have as a part of your belief system one way to install it in your mind is repetition. Then it will be a natural way of thinking and feeling.

I repeat CDs, books, movies, anything that I feel is in alignment with what I want as my core beliefs. I want to naturally think and act from certain thoughts and beliefs. The more I hear it, the more it is a part of who I am, automatically.

"I appreciate what I have in my life now. It has served me. I am so grateful for what is coming!"

Another way to install new thoughts and beliefs in your subconscious is through hypnosis, and meditation. I have many audios that help you do this. It's the easy, natural and joyful way to install positive, powerful new thoughts and beliefs. That is how you create your own reality! Try it, you'll feel great!

My friend and author, Dr. Joe Vitale wrote in his blog about the negative press and "controversy" that has arisen since the movie has become so popular.

"It has now become so popular that critics and nay sayers who want to rain on anyone's parade who is happy and positive have come out. And I'd make sure people knew that feeling is more important than thought in creating your own reality."

"By creating a life worth living, I make a difference in the world -- first in my own life, and then in the lives of others who are inspired to dare something worthy, too." Joe Vitale

I do not have any interest in getting into the nay sayers, but I want to mention that the Law of attraction is not about blame, it is about empowerment. What some people are seeing as dis-empowering is actually the exact opposite...the 'Secret' shows that YOU are the only one who has the power to create your life the way you want it. Do you see what this means? This is a GREAT thing! You have control of your life and everything in it! That means you do not have to be a victim or feel powerless. You can decide to learn how it works, apply it, let love into your heart and take action on what you want. Now you can learn the rules and apply them to win the game your way.

"I am so grateful for my body, my mind and my endless supply of Divine energy."

I have attracted so many things into my life; love, gifts, money, fun, trips, people, friends, business, direction, meaning, healing, joy...it never ends! I know that you can create, or rather uncover the life of your dreams. It is already here. I am pleased to share the tools I know to make it easy and fun to create your life the way you want it! So whether it is a movie like "The Secret", "what the Bleep do we know", a book, or audio, repeat the positive, empowering messages till you believe it. Watch it, enjoy it, share it with your kids and friends. Create a group of people around you who are intentional in living their lives, it is so much fun! Being around like minded people is vital to your happiness and success in creating your reality the way you like it to be.

Live an inspiring life!

So when using your energy systems, realize that getting your energy all in the same 'belief' and all working together, you can really power up your affirmations. Money loves speed, and manifesting will speed up when you align your energy. Use the words to create a picture, or vision and engage your mind. Increase passion, and engage your emotions and other systems. Then live in it mentally and feel it more deeply until it becomes a part of your heart. Once it feels normal and real to you, you have aligned your vibration to what you want, and it will appear. You must do this even before you see anything.

MAGNETIC WEALTH AFFIRMATIONS FOR STEPPING INTO YOUR MASTERY

- I am a powerful creator. I accept my Divine creative abilities and allow them to guide my life.
- I am so grateful for my body, my mind and my endless supply of Divine energy.
- I choose what I put into my mind. I repeat only empowering, positive and possibility filled thoughts.
- I appreciate what I have in my life now. It has served me. I am so grateful for what is coming!
- I ask for what I want with clear vision.
  I expect what I have asked for with total faith.
  I claim what is already here for me with absolute joy.
  Thank you Thank You Thank you.

"YOUR BODY IS LITERALLY A VORTEX OF ENERGY, A CONDUIT THROUGH WHICH DIVINE CREATIVE ENERGY FLOWS AND IS DIRECTED BY YOU INTO WHATEVER FORM YOU WANT.

YOU ARE A CO-CREATOR OF YOUR WORLD, OF THE WORLD."

- NAN AKASHA

Do Affirmations Work?

Chapter 2

"To be ambitious for wealth and yet always expecting to be poor, to be forever doubting your ability to get what you long for, is like trying to reach east by traveling west."
- Og Mandino

Do affirmations work? This is such an interesting question. Have you asked it? Have you pondered it?

I have used affirmations for 23 years. I have used them diligently, daily, and also hardly at all. I have repeated them verbally, said them into a mirror, recorded them on an audio and played them as I fell asleep. I have hand written them over and over. I have printed them and pasted them on my walls, mirrors and doors. I am a big believer in repetition. It works.

So... do they work? YES! For some... not at all for most. The way I was taught and the way affirmations are usually used, they are not powerful at all. Most people see little to no results. It can be a so so tool, or it can be a powerful tool. You have to learn how to make them magnetic and do them in a way that connects to energy.

Even in the traditional way, affirmations have wonderful qualities that I use to enhance other tools I utilize. It needs a boost though. Hence, the birth of magnetic affirmations.

Affirmations alone will get you what you want, you just may be real old when you get it! However, there is a way to pump up the volume. I ask more of a tool, because I want extraordinary results. How powerful fast, easy and fun are they? That is my criteria, right? Fun, easy, quick.

"I am magnetic to all I desire."

So when you look at tools you use to create your reality, what do you look for? Do they create miracles, or just help you see the path to the door you want to open? Do you have to say them out loud, or write them down? To get really great results do you have to visualize or feel them? Do you have to repeat them over and over, many times a day? Are they make believe, or something to do to make you feel better?

Keys to a supercharged affirmation

Here's the keys to a supercharged affirmation, one that works. First you have to know how to use it and when. What it means and what your intent, focus is. Why are you using affirmations? What outcome did you think it would help you achieve? Because you want something to change. Because you want something you don't have (more money, a car...), you don't want something you do have (extra weight, a bad habit...). Get clear! Make sure you are focused on what you do want, not what you don't.

What is your end result? What do you want to feel like? What do you want to BE, do, have?

Are your affirmations empty, not working, lacking passion?

An affirmation is a seed, or what I call a statement of limitless potential. It is specifying the essence, feeling and experience you desire, and it helps you focus, and tune in to it. It is crafting a way of saying, seeing and feeling what you wish to have, be or do.

A certain inner landscape is optimal for affirmations. You want to feel good when using one. You must believe it will work. Know it will help you clarify. *Begin to tune in to how it will feel and be when this is your current reality.* If you do it to make something happen and you just repeat it over and over and hope something shows up, you have diluted it's power. You must work on suspending your disbelief long enough to start to let yourself imagine. Pretend what it will feel like and get it clear in your mind.

"I deserve all the good things the world has to offer."

You must know what your purpose is in saying one. It's not to make it happen, it is to tune YOU to it. It is already there, remember? You want to reveal it, and you do that by getting next to it. It is to make it clear, refine the details, merge with the feeling, see it and get excited about it coming.

An affirmation is the tunnel you can walk thru, that defines the space within which you create the 'practice' of moving into it. You create your reality by *living in to* the life you want. An affirmation guides the way, it enhances your feelings of it, it reminds you of what you asked for and to look for it, feel it. You are tuning in to an experience that is out there and this helps you tune your dial to the same frequency.

"I choose I can Believe, Receive, and Achieve now."

You can make an affirmation more powerful. To me I never use them alone. They take too long. If you are doing repetitive reading, saying or writing of an affirmation, I wish you would ask yourself why? Yes, some repetition is good, even required. But what is your reason and energy behind repeating? Make sure you check on your energy and intent, see if this is why;

- Do you not believe it will work and so you want to be keep asking?
- Are you afraid the Universe has not heard you? Doesn't really know what you want? (I used to think that one!)
- Here is a really common mistake; repeating from desperation. I know from my own experience, repeating something, initially, or perhaps a long time later for a tune up so to speak, is a great way to use affirmations. But repeating from

desperation, worry, lack of trust, or thinking this has to be hard work, will not enhance or help you at all. You are giving off an energy of distrust and you are saying "I don't think you heard me, or I don't think I deserve to be heard, or I need to clear so you really know what I want". Lack of trust is a repelling energy. We want to exude inviting energies. Attractive energies.

"An affirmation is a tool to help you move into the feeling of having and being what you desire."

Magnetic Process:

So you speed up the manifestation time when you say it with feeling. Practice feeling it, seeing and smelling it. Let the power and energy of the word, images and concepts wash through you. Use your senses. Feel it in different parts of your body.

This is *full body affirmation!*

- Act, walk, hold yourself like your affirmation...like the person you have to BE in order for this to become your reality.
- Say it while feeling your energy moving out to draw in the exact things, people, situations, connections you require to make manifest your idea. If it's dry, painful or feels like work and boring, stop it! It isn't helping.

**The only time I do recommend doing affirmations when they feel uncomfortable, is when you are first moving into a reality you have not been familiar with much. Like saying I love you into the mirror (or at all). Or telling yourself you are beautiful and have a slender, sexy body when all you are seeing is your current out of shape one. I do think there is benefit in doing this just for the power in getting comfortable saying it. You desensitize yourself to the negative reaction within you over this positive affirmation. Then you can get to neutral. If you are so disconnected and embarrassed by it, this is a great way to start. Especially if you want more money and you feel really scared asking for it or believing you are worth asking a bigger fee or salary for practice saying it till it does not make you cringe or shrink away. until your inner talk shuts up and stops saying "yeah, right".

"My word has power, my mind is my ally."

Many years ago I went to a monthly meeting where they taught many wonderful things. One day I was sitting in the 3rd row, and the teacher said "we are going to go around the room, one by one, and each person will say "I love ___" and then their own name. You do not have to stand up, simply say it out loud when it comes to your turn." I immediately began to sweat. I had very low self esteem and I had been rigorously taught to never be vain, put myself first or say anything that made me look good/better than others. I had never, ever said I loved myself. This triggered immense fear and massive discomfort. I knew I could not do it. As they went along the first row, I was sweating and thinking madly how I could leave the room. As they went through the second row of people I began to shake, literally. My whole body was going into a massive fight or flight mode and I could not think straight.

I honestly do not remember what I did! I don't know if I said it that day or not, but what I do remember is how that fear shocked and amazed me. It brought to my attention how deeply disconnected I was from myself. How much I truly needed to be able to not only say I loved myself, but really love myself. It started me on a journey that continues today, into deeper and deeper self love and acceptance.

"Affirmations bring me clarity, clarity beings me energy, energy brings reality."

I am proud to say I can say I love myself anytime, anywhere and really mean it now! However, it was a process... and that process may begin with simply saying an affirmation that makes you feel uncomfortable as well. Just say it until you no longer get upset, uncomfortable or hear your inner critic saying "not for me". Then when you get to neutral, you can really start to manifest!

Magnetic Process:

How to make an affirmation Magnetic

In order to really make your affirmation magnetic, powerful and effective, you must include these components.

1. Know your 'why', your purpose in using the affirmation.

2. See the end result.
3. Enhance the image, add sensory elements.
4. Feel how you will feel when this is true for you
5. Write, say out loud, repeat the affirmation when you are fully present and pay attention to how it feels and where you feel it.
6. Pump up the volume on the energy and passion
7. Repeat with Faith, trust and expectation.
8. Look for it to appear, watch for proof and celebrate it!

Secret Key to Master Your Money Mind: In order to create and attract anything into your life it takes

- Laser FOCUS
- Profound Belief
- Full Sensory Imagery

Ways to use affirmations

1. Write them and put where you can see them often (mirror, car, fridge).
2. Say them out loud.
3. Record them onto an audio and play back. Repeat them when awake, driving, doing dishes. Play as you fall asleep, and while you are asleep.
4. Hand write them 3x and then look at them until it is imprinted on your mind.
5. Make mini posters on colored paper, and print them and put on walls, in office etc.
6. Make a song from them that rhymes and becomes like a jingle in your head and sing to yourself.
7. Write on back of business cards and carry in wallet and take out regularly to look at and repeat.
8. Write on post it notes and stick up on phone, desk, fridge, car mirror or dash, bathroom mirror, back of bathroom door, so you see when you close it and are.
9. Sitting, inside your day planner, journal or calendar.
10. Make a habit of reminding yourself of your current affirmation when you go to the bathroom or open doors, something you know you do several times a day.
11. Put it into your electronic calendar, as a daily reminder, so it pops up once or more a day.
12. Send yourself an email with it plus encouraging thoughts.
13. Send yourself a card with the affirmation and congratulations in the mail.
14. Read them just prior to going to sleep and when you wake up.

15. Look at and say an affirmation just as you begin to meditate and let it guide your meditation and vision.
16. Put it on a vision board or in a vision journal.
17. Make a "Mind Movie" or other video with pictures, music and the affirmation, all things that bring up emotion and anticipation.
18. State your affirmation just before you go into a meeting, event, or anything where you want to empower yourself.
19. Use the "why am I so..." statement and then go out into your day looking for proof (You take an affirmation, like " I am an uplifting person and people love to hire me" and change it into "Why am I such an uplifting person? "Why do people love to hire me?" and let the Universe bring you answers!)

When I am in bed, I look at them, read them and feel them as I go to sleep. I do the same when I wake up. Going to sleep while feeling and visualizing an affirmation is very powerful. Whenever you can get past the conscious mind, you are programming into the subconscious mind and this is a much more direct way.

"I know what I want and ask for it with gratitude and expectation."

Saying an affirmation over has a little power, but it has to break through the wall of the conscious mind, which is usually way too busy yacking away to listen. This is why doing an affirmation as you begin to meditate and then letting it guide your meditation, is also very effective, and really fun. To me it is like getting on a train ride and riding into the unknown. I love to see where I go in the meditation. Asking a question that will help guide you to knowing more about the path to your desire empowers an affirmation too.

So I want to end by sharing some of my affirmations that came true, and often in amazing ways. You may have read I moved to Austin last year. Well, 2-3 years before, I plastered the word "Austin", that I cut out from magazines, all over my vision board. I am amazed it happened because the way I saw and thought I wanted it to happen kind of died out after awhile, and I moved to a new vision board, thinking that had just been what I wanted at the time, and now I had other things I wanted and I let it go. Then, without my remembering, moving to Austin came back into my present reality in a big way, and took over the path of life for many months. It wasn't until I was packing and saw the old vision board that I realized what had happened! I was tickled and amazed.

"I claim my power to create now."

I put up calendars with pictures of Italy and the countryside in Tuscany in my house one year. I did it more because I like to surround myself with beautiful things and I love Italy, and always want to go back. It did not start out with me having any intent of "I am going here this year". So repetition was very unintentional. I had no plans and saw no way of going to Italy that year, and so I was amazed when we got invited to Italy and specifically to spend 2 weeks in a villa on a vineyard in Tuscany. One day, after I began to plan the trip, I walked past one of the calendars and stopped dead. They had been up for 11 months, so I didn't notice them as much. I stood in amazement, just looking at it. I was stunned I had manifested a trip there, without any effort other than having the images in my view daily and appreciating the beauty and wonder of it.

Share yours :)

"I am a master Creator."

MAGNETIC WEALTH AFFIRMATIONS FOR BEING MAGNETIC WHEN YOU USE AFFIRMATIONS

1. I am magnetic to all I desire.
2. I am a powerful manifester.
3. I am what I think about most.
4. I choose I can Believe, Receive, and Achieve now.
5. I deserve all the good things the world has to offer.
6. My word has power, my mind is my ally.
7. Affirmations bring me clarity, clarity beings me energy, energy brings reality.
8. I know what I want and ask for it with gratitude and expectation.
9. I claim my power to create now.
10. I am a master Creator.

"Happiness + Money = Freedom."

- Nan Akasha

DID YOU KNOW YOUR MONEY IS STANDING NEXT TO YOU?

Chapter 3

"You don't become enormously successful without encountering some really interesting problems."
- Mark Victor Hansen

Everyone wants to make more money, right? Yep, even if they won't admit it. It's OK, it's natural. No matter what you were told, wanting to be wealthy is not bad, it is your natural state. You have a natural desire for thriving and abundance and so this is merely you yearning for your Divine state.

Well, the good news is you are wired for wealth. All of your systems in your body, mind and energy field are designed to work with you and for you. The Universe, all the energy around you, is designed to support and create whatever vision you hold. Everything is on your side!

"My money is standing next to me! I claim it!"

What's even better? You are standing right smack dab in the middle of what you want!! Yep! It's *already there*.

Follow this:
1. Everything is energy... even you... even money.

2. Your attraction vibe is your output energy and it determines what you see, experience and live.
3. All possibilities exist *already*, in this and every moment.
4. Align your thoughts with what you WANT, as often as possible, and expand the vision each day.
5. Be clear that your dominant purpose, intent is to "get rich", 'be wealthy", "attract money".
6. Manage your energy: pay attention to where it goes, what you do and think and how you feel. Intend to align with the wealth that is ALREADY HERE!
7. Keep impressing upon your mind that you are already wealthy and you are ready to align with the riches all around you.
8. Do this until it is a habit, a way of feeling, Being and living, that takes no extra energy.

Make it happen

You are in charge, You have to step up and take charge of your thoughts and stay focused. Communicate constantly to your mind and the Universe what you want... or choose now. Be specific about how you prefer it to be and never give up. 90% of failure is from not beginning or giving up. If you begin and never give up your vision or dream and keep moving forward, you will succeed! There's no way you can't, unless you give up or never start.

What would you do if you KNEW you couldn't fail?

Choose wealth now and let go of the struggle!

"I accept my natural divine state of wealth."

I know you want results and change! I know you want to be living the life that makes you smile each day you get up. So support yourself in achieving the success you want and raise your energy, focus your mind, power up your hearts and make it happen! DECIDE.

How I made it Happen

I began real estate investing because I magnetically drew to me what would most serve me. I was not aware, at all, I wanted to have anything to do with Real Estate. I did, however, have a powerful inner desire for something that would interest me, stimulate me, push me to grow, and give me independence and freedom. It showed up in the form of Real Estate investing. I was so drawn to it, it kept showing up over and over. At first I ignored it. Thankfully, the Universe and our minds keep bringing us opportunities that will lead us to what we most desire. Even if we do not recognize it at first.

My mind kept putting it in front of me, over and over, till I paid attention. I kept walking in the bedroom late at night while the TV was on and seeing the same infomercial about investing.

I was raised that you never buy anything on TV, it was tacky. So I did not pay attention, I had a prejudice against it even before I knew what it was. I ignored it the first two times, the third time I watched a bit, the fourth time I watched more and by the seventh day in a row it showed up in my awareness, I finally paid attention. I called up and spent 2 hours on the phone with some sweet man who answered tons of questions and basically counseled me on what to do. My inner voice and all my energy was so incredibly drawn to this. I could not ignore it. I wanted it with all my being, and I also knew it would upset my husband at the time.

"I align my thoughts with what I WANT, in every moment. I expand my vision each day."

Luckily I do follow my inner guidance and I dove in. It was all I wanted to think about and do 24/7... that is passion! It was a huge personal growth experience. Starting with my husband. He was so pissed off, he did not speak to me for two months. I was on my own to begin this huge new venture. I knew inside it was what I was meant to do, so I focused and began to make it happen.

In my first year I encountered problems and people I had no idea existed. I bought 5 houses in one week at the end of the 3rd month in business. I had never rehabbed a house before and so I hired a contractor I met on another site. We agreed on a price, he signed the contract and we got started. All went well for a few weeks and then he stopped showing up. At the time I had no idea this was common for contractors. I called, I left notes at the house, I laid awake at night worrying and stressing out. Finally I got a message from his wife, who I had never met. She claimed he did not feel I had paid him enough, and he would not do anymore work and that he had filed a lien on the property. I freaked out.

"I choose wealth now and let go of the struggle!"

I cried, I complained, I screamed injustice from the rooftops. Did it help? No. Just caused me more stress. I was in shock, he had agreed and I had even made a schedule of payments and had paid him several times already. Finally, I called a friend who had been in this business for a while. He called and tried to talk to his wife, she called him a racist and hung up! (This was one Hispanic to another, so who knows where she got that!!) My head was spinning, my sense of 'fairness' was insulted and I was stunned. My dreams seemed to be dying.

Then I found out that this contractor was famous for doing this! Two very successful and seasoned investors came to me and asked about the situation. When I told them who it was, they explained that this man had done this to both of them, and some others they knew. That his entire M.O. was to start a job, do a great job for a short time and then begin to complain, ask for more money and not show up. They told me no matter what I did, he would not finish, or be 'reasonable'. His intent was to start as many jobs as possible, collect up front money and then stall and look for something to complain about and then file a lien.

I could talk for hours about all the pain, fear, stress and emotional trauma I went through. There was a lot of money on the line, I was new and inexperienced in this business. I lived with a negative, unsupportive spouse who hated my business and was not about to console or help me. My mind would not stop going over the facts and how this person was a liar, and was screwing me over.

"I raise my energy to match my dreams. I can achieve my dreams. I focus my mind, power up my heart and make it happen!"

What happened? Well, in the end, none of these problems stopped me. I made it happen. I worked through my fears, I let go of the sense of injustice and wanting the contractor to do what he promised to do and I asked for help. In the end I had to hire another contractor, and pay an attorney and the first contractor $1000 to drop the lien so I could sell the house (yes, even though he did not 'deserve' it). Was it fair? No. Was it stressful, yes. Did I learn a ton? Most definitely! What was the biggest lesson? (believe me, there were many!!!!) *You get to choose what to do and what to feel about anything that happens.* You get to let go and move on, instead of getting stuck in 'it's not fair'. You get to choose success, despite anyone else. You get to choose, every day, to be a victim or be the master of your reality. It is up to you, like it was up to me.

You get to decide if you are going to let anyone else steal your dreams. I said no!

I learned more mentally, emotionally and spiritually doing Real Estate investing than almost any other thing. It really pushed me out of my comfort zone and made me face my fears. It made me see more of the big picture and most of all... it made me more determined that no one else was going to steal my dreams. I was in charge of my reality and I was going to make it happen. I kept solving problems and moving forward. I was rewarded. The best reward to me though, was the incredible expansion within me. Personal growth is our real prize.

I found strength, focus, and commitment. I found confidence and I increased my tolerance for stress. That means less things stressed me. I saw things more as a step on the path, not the end. I always looked for another way, a solution and I always found a door. I kept saying "no one is keeping me from my dream," and I did what I had to do to achieve it. I stayed true to myself and my vision, and kept moving forward.

"I choose success. I choose to BE the master of my reality."

Make it happen for you. Realize that everything is an opportunity and you can face your fears, get stronger and more centered.

You can make your dreams happen for you. Anything you desire!! Clean up the internal blocks and open to possibilities. I love making it happen!! Isn't it the best thrill in life when something you have desired and focused on happens? You bet it is!! So, do you feel full of possibility? Do you feel like anything is possible and you can have whatever you want?

I know what it feels like to know I am capable and deserving of anything I want, and I know what it feels like to NOT feel like that! We have only one thing that keeps us from having the exact life experience we desire... it is ourselves!

Yes, you are the one stopping you, and you may not even know you are doing it or why! And even more important; are you letting perceived failures, negative people, or outcomes that aren't what you hoped for stop you? Like Mark says in the quote above, success brings with it a whole bunch of interesting 'problems'. Do you let them paralyze you? Achieving what you want has to be worth it to you, because making it happens means letting nothing stop you! Maybe you have not even gotten started in moving towards your goals from fear you don't know how, can't handle what comes up or feel unworthy?

"I AM always aware of my dominant purpose. My intent is to 'get rich', 'be wealthy', 'attract money'."

I have been in business for myself for over 26 years now. I have had 5 different businesses from large to small, from employees to just me. I have pushed past my comfort zone and faced my fears over and over again. I know how to problem solve and how to stay positive, keep moving forward and enjoy the journey. I do not want to see anything stop you from living the life you truly want. I want to help you align your internal world with the external one, so you can experience the kind of joy, happiness, wealth, health and love you deserve! Don't let anyone steal your dream!

I have coached people for over nine years on starting businesses, changing their mindset, releasing the past, attracting money, finding their purpose, creating a real estate investment portfolio and more. I know that life and business especially, brings its challenges. This is when you have to remember "Everything is Opportunity"... and see the gift inside whatever you are experiencing. It always has within it many doors.

"I am wired for wealth. Everything is on my side!"

It is when we hit a wall, when we most need the internal tools and strength and support to move onward. It is in knowing the laws and rules of the game, of your mind and energy, understanding other people and aligning with our selves that gives us the knowing of what to do and when to do it. Choose to believe in yourself, and choose other beliefs that support you. Then when you hit the rough spots, you have these to fall back on. Money is standing next to you, and all other things you truly desire. It is your choice to decide you deserve them and you will not let anyone or anything stop you.

It is having a guide and someone who believes in us to keep us going when it seems hard. I am here for you. Use magnetic goals and draw financial success to you.

"I love the thrill of allowing my desires to happen. I feel full of possibility. I know anything is possible and I can have whatever I want!"

Keep focused always and only on what you want, do not let what you don't want distract your focus.

Your personal commitment to yourself and your dreams is vital. Money, love, health, anything you feel you want to desire, is standing next to you. First you have to decide you want it, and you will not let anything keep you from it. This creates an energetic bond. The strength of your decision, with your vision and your persistent action brings goodies. One of my favorite phrases is "When you are willing to do the work, you get the goodies!" Never fails.

Ask yourself again:

"If I KNOW I cannot fail, what would I be doing right now!"

Your money is standing next to you, what do you say to it? What are you willing to do to meet it, build rapport with it, choose it, claim it?

Magnetic Wealth Affirmations for claiming the Money Standing right next to you

- My money is standing next to me! I claim it!
- I accept my natural divine state of wealth
- I am wired for wealth. Everything is on my side!
- I align my thoughts with what I WANT, in every moment. I expand my vision each day
- I AM always aware of my dominant purpose. My intent is to 'get rich', 'be wealthy", 'attract money'.
- I choose wealth now and let go of the struggle!
- I raise my energy to match my dreams. I can achieve my dreams. I focus my mind, power up my heart and make it happen!
- I DECIDE. I support my decisions with joyful vision and absolute faith that what I want is already here!
- I choose success. I choose to BE the master of my reality.
- I AM strength, focus, and commitment. I claim my confidence and increase my tolerance for stress.
- I stay true to myself and my vision. I keep moving forward.
- I love the thrill of allowing my desires to happen. I feel full of possibility. I know anything is possible and I can have whatever I want!
- I am capable and deserving of anything.
- I make my dreams happen, now!

"I NOW COMMIT TO MY DREAMS. I DECIDE TO
MAKE THEM HAPPEN, HERE AND NOW, FOR
ME."

- NAN AKASHA

OUR MIND: GATEWAY TO REALITY

Chapter 4

*"All riches, of whatever nature, begin
as a state of mind."*
- Napoleon Hill

Your mind is energy, just like all of you and all of reality. Your mind is the filter through which you see, create and experience your life. There is a reason I say "free your mind and the wealth will follow". So will the love, joy, happiness and anything else, if you are willing to master your mind.

Who is in your mind? Most people are not in their own mind. They let others in and they think based on what others tell them is right for them. They are literally 'out' of their mind. This means creating by default. Most people get caught in a loop in the small logical mind and do not take command of their creative mind.

You are not in control of your mind if you are drifting... in fear, worry or some other emotion. Something like 80% or more of our thoughts are unproductive and repetitive. When you are not intentional about your mind, someone else is in your mind choosing for you. When you do not consciously choose what is allowed in your mind and what it looks for, you cannot expect to live in a reality of your choosing. Is that what you really want?

Your mind creates, filters, seeks and interprets. It is your control panel of your life. BE in your mind. How? BE in the present moment! How? Think about your belly button. Really, it will bring you right into the now. Then assess how you feel and what you are thinking about.

Another way we let others into our minds is by worrying about what others think. Seeking approval, worrying that someone will not agree with or like your actions, thoughts or choices, is giving away your power. Start now to see who is thinking or influencing the thinking in your mind. I realized one day several years ago, that my husband and my dad were always in my mind, monitoring my thinking. Now I am not saying they were doing it, I am saying, I was allowing it. I was so attached to what they thought and how they reacted to what I did, that all my decisions had these two background voices giving their opinions.

"My money is natural, automatic, easy, flowing, fun, light, and happy. So AM I."

Every time I was shopping for anything, even groceries or other necessities, I would hear them giving their criticism. I would often stress because I would worry what they were going to say when I got home or was asked what I bought. My ex husband's first thing he would say to me when I came home, was "how much did you spend?". Not 'how are you', 'how was your day', 'I love you' or even a hug. I knew there was criticism coming to me from all three of them on almost everything I did. Because it mattered to me, and I still wanted their love, and approval, this was a constant stress and really ruined my relationship with money. It is hard to feel abundant, limitless, free and full of potential when you have this hanging over your head!

That was a huge realization, and an empowering moment when I took back my power by kicking all others out of my mind. Do this and see how free you feel, how much easier it is to tune in to your true Soul desires, your Soul's plan.. Authentic. Tune in to your authentic self and let that be what fills and guides your mind. <u>Reclaiming your own authority to yourself is needed to feel worthy enough to attract wealth.</u>

Magnetic Process:

So as you create your Wealth mindset (contact me if you are interested in a custom made Wealth mindset script and audio), be aware of who is in your mind. We all let others in to our minds at some point, and being aware of it will shift your energy and power back to you. Get your journal and ask yourself "Who is in my mind?". "Who makes my decisions?"

One more note; when we are growing up, our minds are wide open. We absorb most others beliefs, and so as adults we have to realize, remove and choose new ones that support us.

Wealth starts in your mind!

The energetic system that we call our mind is a miracle in action every day, every moment. Our mind is multi-dimensional and each part has a different function. I love to study and discover the power of our minds. It is, to me, the gateway to our reality.

Our mind is:

- the frame through which we filter everything.
- our experience of life.
- a problem solving mechanism.
- always listening.
- the cockpit from which you captain yourself.
- where you create the vision that becomes your life.

Our mind listens to what we say, feel and see in our minds eye. Our mind communicates in pictures. Our mind is watching what we repeat the most often with the most passion, and then makes that a priority. It makes you aware of whatever you have 'told' it is most important to you. It is solving the problem, attracting the resources and anything else... all the time.

> "It's only a thought, and
> a thought can be changed."
> - Louise Hay

Changing your life by changing your thoughts works. By being aware of what you think. By choosing what you think and learning how your mind works.

We have the ability to choose our thoughts, however most people simply go through life without being present or aware. Wondering why they don't get what they want or can't achieve sustainable success. Granted, few of us are taught how powerful our thoughts are, or how to be the master of our minds. The reality is, if we give priority to knowing what we are thinking, and begin to consciously choose what we want to think, we can create massive, positive change in our lives!

"I think what I WANT regardless of what is appearing around me. I believe in me."

Our mind is a tool. An amazing, programmable one that supports us. What we 'feed' it, what we ask it for, how we ask and how consistently we communicate determines our experience of life each day. Imagine being able to think what you WANT, when you want. Not feeling like your emotions are running away with your thoughts. Don't let your emotions control you. This is easier than you think.

"Success in life comes from being willing to move into Unchartered Territory. Life begins at the end of your Comfort Zone."
- Neale Donald Walsch

Change what you believe to change your life

We have to change what we believe in order to change what kind of life we have. What we think and therefore believe determines our mood, our wealth, our love... anything we get to have in our lives. This is "only a thought, and a thought can be changed" Louise Hay says. You had to choose the thoughts you have now. You weren't born with them downloaded into you. You chose them and now you can change what you choose. Change what you think of most often, and then change what you think it means. These are the power places.

Align with the Best Mentally

When you decide to think a certain way and act from it, you have taken charge of your reality. You can literally decide to think anything you want, and you can choose what it means. What it means to you, about you and about the world. I personally like to think the most loving, inspiring, uplifting, empowering and strengthening thoughts. I have created a habit of thinking the best, of myself, of others, of the situation. *I intentionally align myself with the best.*

"I create massive, positive change in my life through empowering thoughts!"

Use your mind to create habits. This makes life easy, and fun. Habits are easy to create, you simply repeat behavior, thoughts over each day for 30 -60 days and you have created a new neural pathway in your brain! Support what you want by making it a priority, interrupting negative and unsupported thoughts and deciding to believe whatever gives you the most energy, love, happiness, confidence and passion.

Wealth is your natural state. Feel your way back to it. See it in your mind daily. Live in your wealthy life mentally. Invite your true Wealthy Inner Being to come out and play.

Magnetic Process:

Embody, embrace, exude wealth

Here you first feel the BEingness of wealth by embodying it. It comes from within you, it is you. Imagine how it really feels to BE wealthy and ground it into your cells. Then to embrace it, you open to it (imagine opening your arms) and claim it by pulling it in to you and loving it. Then you give off the vibration of BEing wealth by exuding it. Imagine it being your dominant vibration and radiating out from you at all times. See it being the feeling that attracts to you. BE IT.

This is a simple, yet energetically magnetic and powerful magnetic affirmation. Close your eyes and really feel the different vibration of each state. Say it 3 x, slowly, over. Here you can really see how you BE, you accept, and you give out, it is flow and movement.

"I embody wealth. I embrace wealth. I exude wealth."

Free Your Mind and the Wealth will Follow

Wealth is a state of mind. So is health, freedom and happiness. Ready to FREE your MIND?

I know how the mind works and it is a system. When we know how to use it and tune in to our energy field and the field of abundance all around and within us (as in the 'Force' in Star Wars), we have so much power. This is power that does not require our will power, or effort or even a long time and struggle. When we learn to work with our mind and these systems, they can take over the 'hard' work. If we can get out of our own way, we will find all the solutions come through us with ease.

If you worry about making the right decision, you are not letting your inner systems do their work. They are solving problems for you. You decide what you want and then keep the end result firmly in mind. Then let your mind work with the Universe to show you the path.

In reality you make a decision, and then *you* make it the right one. You do this by believing it, choosing it and supporting it with thoughts and actions every day. You know within you what is right and so you decide, always, no one else. Choose your decision than let go of ever doubting it. Focus on supporting it, making it happen, and making it the right one. Know it is the right one. Your mind, and the Universe & field of abundance will see your commitment and make it happen. Work in concert with all that loves and supports you. Decide that is true for you, and it will be. It is.

"I claim my own authority. I feel worthy enough to attract wealth."

Imagine what it would be like if you really had a free mind! What does that mean? Freeing your mind, to me, is about letting go of fear and worry. Letting go of others opinions. Letting go of constant chatter in your mind about negative things that suck all your energy. Stopping the flow of negative "what if's". It means having a mind that is in your control...not one that is running away with fearful fantasy's and distracting you.

It is so important to me that people get free from fear and false beliefs. It is so vital to having a life you love and enjoy. I talk about money a lot, but don't make the mistake of thinking that means I think money is the most important thing... not by any stretch of the imagination!

In fact we are so bound up in our emotions and beliefs over money. So many people think that by talking about money it means you are superficial, not spiritual and don't care about others! What a load of crap! Why would anyone want money, just to have money? Silly! That would be like saying you want sticks, just because they are sticks. It really is no different. Money in and of itself is nothing but energy. We decide what it means to us.

I want SOOOOO much for you to get this: freedom from money issues and worries is a step into freeing your mind and living a life of love, joy and inner peace! Being happy and feeling good are ALWAYS our motivation. We never do anything except if we think it will avoid pain or get us pleasure. Period. So what I am doing with my classes and coaching is finding the BEST ways to help you free your mind. Free yourself from the ties that bind you around money.

"I claim freedom from money issues. I free my mind and live a life of love, joy and inner peace!"

You may even have money and still have some issues around it. If you would clear those... imagine how amazing you would feel! You could enjoy your life, your wealth, your loved ones, your business, your vacations... all with more presence and feeling! Freeing your mind is about freeing up the energy you waste on worry and fear. Freeing up your energy and time spent wondering and worrying, gives you more ability to be in the moment and savor the richness of your life experience! That is what life is all about. Really being fully present, mind, body and spirit, in all that you do. Seeing and feeling the wonderful sensations of life and being strong, energetic and calm enough to really capture the moment and merge with it.

Life is meant to be fun, joyful, and happy.

We all seek that, no matter what else you have heard. We are not here to suffer, be tested, learn any particular lesson (unless you choose to) or undo wrongs or even pay back karma! We are MASTERS! We are the creators of the world! We are the ones who actually create all that you see and experience! Being the master of your life means easily creating your own reality, right now. You are doing it anyway! Why not be conscious about it? Take that awareness and go deeply into your feelings and experiences! When you feel pain, worry, joy or any emotions, go into it! Go into it like an explorer! Be the master of your life, free your mind and merge with your life in a whole new way!

Free your mind; it will give you unbounded energy, clarity, focus and joy like you have never experienced!

MAGNETIC WEALTH AFFIRMATIONS FOR FREEING YOUR MIND AND OPENING THE GATEWAY TO YOUR REALITY

- I AM in control of my mind. I Am in the present moment and aware of all opportunities.
- I claim my own authority. I feel worthy enough to attract wealth.
- My mind is filled with wealthy, wonderful. thoughts and I enjoy and join every one of them
- I change my life by changing my thoughts. I AM aware of what I think. I choose my thoughts easily.
- My money is natural, automatic, easy, flowing, fun, light, and happy. So AM I.
- I tell my mind repeatedly my top priorities.
- I create massive, positive change in my life through empowering thoughts!
- I think what I WANT regardless of what is appearing around me. I believe in me.
- I claim freedom from money issues. I free my mind and live a life of love, joy and inner peace!
- I embody wealth. I embrace wealth. I exude wealth.

"Wealth is not a single thought, it is a habit.

You are wealthy because of what you repeatedly think."

- Nan Akasha

YOU ARE FREE - WE ALL LIVE LIFE ON OUR OWN "PLANET"

Chapter 5

"...understand that your life can be as wonderful or as horrible as you allow it to be. It all depends upon the thoughts that you practice. And therein lies the basis of anyone's success: How much do I practice thoughts that bring me joy, and how much do I practice thoughts that bring me pain?"

- Abraham Hicks--San Francisco, 3/8/03

You are free, whether you believe it or not. Whether you feel it or not. Even when you are in a situation you perceive limits you, you always have the freedom within to choose how you feel. You have the freedom to decide how you feel, what you think and what you decide things mean. When you pull your energy back in from feeding the past, and the pain, and from people who do not support, respect and uplift you, you are free.

Do not seek approval, validation and too much advice from others. You know what is best for you and the best way to begin to feel free is to make yourself your own best authority. Gather information, learn and practice, but make your own decisions, based on what is best for you. Give yourself the approval and validation you seek from others and it will never go away. Others cannot spend enough of their time and energy on you to keep you happy. They have their own selves to take care of too. We are all living from within our own world, our own perception, perspective, essentially our own 'planet'.

"I choose the atmosphere on MY planet. I now remove what I no longer want on my planet and add what I choose. My Planet supports me in every way."

In our quest to "Create Our Own Realities"... I like the metaphor that we all live on our own planets. In a sense we are each of us a separate self contained planetary system. Planets each have their own characteristics, atmosphere, look, feel, boundaries, laws and so on. They rotate in their own orbit and they interact with other systems/planets, but still remain independent in how they function. So do we!

We create the life/reality/movie we play in called our lives. A friend of mine uses the visual of each of us being our own planet. I really like this! It is easy to understand how we all create our own reality with that concept. We create the characteristics of our lives, our 'planet', through our thoughts and beliefs. Our past experiences and memories color our view, our atmosphere and then things on our planet (in our lives) follows suit. Since no one else, anywhere in the universe, has experienced things in the same way as we have, our "Planet" is unique! Our thoughts, past experiences and beliefs we have formed, all go into creating the unique point of view on our "Planet". No one else has lived our life, felt our feelings or savored our joys. We have to be in charge of our lives, no one else knows us better.

Ever notice how differently each person sees, remembers and experiences something? Ever retell a conversation only to have someone else who was there, remember something different from you? Ever been at a movie, or sports event, or go to a party and then talk about it with someone else who was there? They had a totally different experience than you! This is because we all have formed our thoughts and beliefs from our own personal experience and what we decided it all meant. I might see something as fun and positive and someone else may see that same thing as negative and annoying, merely because they had a different experience of it.

"I carefully choose what is true on my planet and what I agree with. I claim wealth, health, happiness and love in abundance."

Certainly we can see this with age differences. When my daughters say they don't like what I like, or think something is boring that I think is exciting, it is simply our own points of view.

Here's an example: I was in a car accident once and there were 7 witnesses. When the police report was done, all 7 people thought something different had happened, blamed someone different and felt the timing of the events was even different.

One of my favorite experiences is when I talk to someone and they are on a planet that is so different than mine, that they don't even hear or comprehend what I say. I was at a resort once, sitting in the jacuzzi with a loved one. We began to talk to a couple and got into the "what do you do" conversation. We talked excitedly about creating books and audios that increase prosperity consciousness. You could see that we might as well be speaking Chinese to this couple. Not only did that topic hold no interest to them, they literally blanked out and looked and acted like we had not said anything. It was not a part of their reality, thoughts or interests. They knew nothing of intentionally creating, or prosperity consciousness. They went through life doing what they thought they should. This is what one of my mentors called 'Sheeple'. Intentional prosperity was not a part of the atmosphere of their personal energy system; their "Planet".

"I AM Free. Free to choose, free to love, free to embrace the wealthy, healthy, happy being I truly Am. I claim my freedom now!"

People who complain and blame create more of that on their planet because they give it time, energy, attention and then they talk about it with others looking for agreement. When they get others to agree with their limited or angry perspective, they add more magnetic power to that idea and more of it is attracted to them. Whether they realize it or not, everyone has created everything in their lives. Each one of us has created the atmosphere and laws of nature that are 'true' on our planet, in our lives.

There are also things that I do not put any attention on in my life, therefore they do not exist on my Planet Nan. These include war, violence, blame, negative reinforcement and such. I am careful of what I put into my mind and energy. I do not watch the news, and I do not allow those ideas to dwell in my mind. I do not spend time with negative people and I do not agree with people anymore just to be polite. If it is not something I want to be true for me, I do not agree. Agreeing invites it into my reality.

Magnetic Process:

Decide what you want your "Planet" to be Like

Decide what you want your life to be like, and then use it as a template to assess whatever is in or comes in to your life. You have already created life on your 'planet', now it's time to consciously choose what to keep and what to add.

On "Planet Nan" we are happy and loving and self empowered. The atmosphere is about fun, happiness, creativity, business, health and fully expressing ourselves. We are all wealthy and deserve it. Many things do not even show up in my life, even though I am walking in the same city as so many others who do have those things show up in their lives. Abraham Hicks, from the original "The Secret" movie, says to literally ignore what you do not like and want in your life and you will not attract it into your life.

"I inspire money to flow to me. I am inspired to create my life with ease and grace. I allow the river of wealth to carry me, gently and joyfully."

My friend who coined the idea of each of us being our own planet says "Not on my Planet" when people say limiting things and try to include her in it. It stops people in their tracks, and they get it, even if this is a new concept for them. You ever have people at work complain about their kids, spouse, job, life? Ever hear them say things like "Don't you hate it when...?" fill in the blank or "You know what I mean..." or "You know how people always...?"

Next time someone says something negative, complaining, limiting or blaming, try saying "Maybe that is true for you, but not on planet Nan" (well, use your name of course!). They may be a little shocked, but they get it. It is a nice, humorous way to get a very powerful point across... YOU create your reality. Life on YOUR planet is the way you choose it to be, and only you can decide what to include. This is powerful, remember and use this metaphor. It gives you the awareness that we each perceive everything through our own set of very unique filters. These are our thoughts, beliefs (which are thoughts you repeat so often they become automatic) and memories.

What is life like on your planet? Is that something you want to claim as true for you? Is that the climate you want on your planet? Not me! We think it is polite and friendly to agree, yet then we are telling ourselves, our minds and the Universe this is true for us. Be careful what you agree with, be choosy what you claim for yourself.

"The purpose of life is to be happy. I Am living and creating the best life ever. Free, fun, loving, adventurous. Doing what makes me feel good. Yes, yes yes."

What is life like on your planet? You get to choose, you are free to create the rules, and reality on your planet.

On planet Nan, we:
- Have fun all the time.
- Are happy.
- Love ourselves.
- Uplift and inspire ourselves and others.
- Believe we deserve wealth, health and joy.
- Know we create our own reality and we choose our thoughts and words so they create what we want, not what we don't.
- Know well being is the truth.
- Surround ourselves with unconditional love
- Know EVERYTHING IS OPPORTUNITY.
- Know our riches exist in our mind, so we 'mine' them.
- Ask for what we want, expect to receive it, claim that which we have asked for.
- Are always willing to change, grow and face our fears because we know this brings the GOODIES!
- Allow others to be who they choose to be, even our children and respect everyone as Divine beings on their chosen path.

- Surround ourselves with positive, powerful, loving people.
- Release the past, forgive and move on.
- Live a dance between the now moment and creating and living in the future in our minds
- Are loved, loving and loveable.
- Honor our preferences.
- Embrace our personal inner power.
- Enjoy life and live adventure.
- Believe money is our friend and ally and cash flows to us endlessly.

Chris, my beloved, has a wonderful view of life. It is such a joy to live with someone who is always happy, loving, appreciative and allowing.

He creates life on his planet the way he wants. He believes...

- the purpose of life is to be HAPPY.
- he believes that you should have fun at whatever you do.
- He believes in cultivating a prosperous mindset.
- he believes in doing what you love and diversifying.
- he believes you always focus on what you want, not what you don't.

Chris has created a book about how to create new business ideas (or ideas about other things) by playing games. See? Fun! His book called "Play Prosperity Games" is full of processes, and games on generating ideas from things you love and love to do. It gives you a way to put ideas together that your logical mind would not normally do. You combine things that would make no sense at all in ordinary circumstances.

Not only has he created this fun and inspiring book, but he has done speaking events, dinner parties and workshops where you actually get to play the games. You have a blast as you match up things you love to do and brainstorm with the other people there. He has a bonus report on how to throw your own party!

"I play prosperity games every day. Prosperity is my natural state and the more fun I have the more wealth comes to me!"

Very interactive, very experiential. You walk away with ideas you can use. Many people so far have bought website names right away from their ideas.

I have been to many of them, it was a blast! I had so much fun helping others and was amazed when I got one idea (among many others) that I am already researching on how to implement. You *will* leave with ideas... everyone has!

It is like turning on a faucet of ideas too! They keep pouring into you after you start playing these games. It is like it starts your creative flow. You just have to be aware, watch for the ideas, watch for the people, opportunities and resources that start to appear. Be prepared for fun and be ready to take action, you will get great inspiration.

You can see all about his book and get it if you are inspired at www.PlayProsperityGames.com

So you can see how Chris' personal beliefs effect how he thinks, what he does and how he lives on his planet. He incorporates his belief of having fun and doing what you love into a business. He attracts ideas on other business ideas and for making websites for clients, all that align with his personal atmosphere. You can too.

MAGNETIC WEALTH AFFIRMATIONS FOR BEING FREE & LIVING LIFE ON YOUR OWN "PLANET"

- I choose the atmosphere on MY planet. I now remove what I no longer want on my planet and add what I choose. My Planet supports me in every way.
- I carefully choose what is true on my planet and what I agree with. I claim wealth, health, happiness and love in abundance.
- I AM Free. Free to choose, free to love, free to embrace the wealthy, healthy, happy being I truly Am. I claim my freedom now!
- The purpose of life is to be happy. I Am living and creating the best life ever. Free, fun, loving, adventurous. Doing what makes me feel good. Yes, yes yes.
- I play prosperity games every day. Prosperity is my natural state and the more fun I have the more wealth comes to me!
- I inspire money to flow to me. I am inspired to create my life with ease and grace. I allow the river of wealth to carry me, gently and joyfully.

"TO EMBODY THE SPIRIT OF MONEY IS TO KNOW A FREEDOM AROUND MONEY THAT MOST OF US HAVE NEVER EXPERIENCED.

FOR MANY PEOPLE, MONEY IS A SOURCE OF STRUGGLE AND CONFLICT, BUT THIS IS TRULY UNNECESSARY.

UNIFYING WITH THE ENERGY SYSTEM CALLED MONEY IS A BLESSED AND SACRED EXPERIENCE, AND IT IS AVAILABLE TO ALL WHO SEEK IT."

NAN AKASHA

YOUR WEALTH VIBE
FOLLOW THE ENERGY

Chapter 6

"What you radiate outward in your thoughts, feelings, mental pictures and words, you attract into your life and daily affairs."
- Catherine Ponder

We are energy. Everything is energy. Money is energy. Your mind is energy. Energy systems, all made of the *same* energy. Wealth is a state of mind, which is energy. Never ending, always moving and vibrating energy. Energy vibrates at different rates in order to appear and function in different ways. You and an apple, and your car, and a dollar bill, and a giraffe and a tree are all made from the *same* substance. Intelligent, Divine, conscious energy.

This energy is all around us, within us and *is* us. I call it the field of abundance. Some people call it Source, The one, God/Goddess, the Divine... in any verbiage it is abundant and intelligent.

"I ALIGN my wealth vibe with my vision and attract all I need to live and make it my reality."

Since we are all made from the same thing, we can transform into anything. We can match up to anything.

We can attract anything. We can be MAGNETIC to anything. (Why BE magnetic? It is about ease! It is easy to let your magnetic nature attract to you what you need to choose the life you want!)

"I am in harmonious flow with the field of abundance."

This field of abundance is in constant flow. The key to attracting what we want, BEing what we want, feeling like we want, is to ALIGN ourselves with it. Since we are energy, then we can shift our vibration, alter our frequency and thus attract to us what we match this frequency to. In fact it is more like revealing what is already existing, but to us, it seems like a journey. If you take a moment to consider that we are all made up of energy, the interconnectedness of all energies becomes evident.

Money is nothing more than energy that we experience in the form of paper, coins and electrons. Money can even appear digitally or virtually... like stocks, or online bank accounts. And in the same sense that we can connect with any other form of energy, we can also connect directly with the Spirit of Money.

"I AM Divine creative Energy. Money is Divine creative Energy. We are one."

Relaxation is key to our happiness, success and creativity. Relax in to your energy and let it carry you.

Don't measure your success, wealth, life by what you are currently experiencing physically around you. Measure it by what is going on within you! Your inner world is always ahead of your outer world. Manifestation is a process, it can be fast or slow, yet it always IS... meaning it is always happening. Energy is always moving, creation is always happening, and just because you do not see it with your physical eyes does not mean it is not there!

"I now choose to allow my desires, intentions, thoughts and energy to align. I flow forward with ease and grace."

We can see very little in the scope of things with our physical eyes. This is not the way to assess what your reality is. Insects can see more than we can, dogs can hear things we can't. Our body is just one part of our multi dimensional beingness. Therefore it is not only vital, but freeing and delicious, when we embrace the WHOLENESS of who we are. When we tune into energy, especially our own energies, a new world opens up. More information, guidance, and possibility. We then experience our lives on the multiple levels it is actually occurring.

Trust yourself. You know the answers, you have the help and you are supported by all. There is well being within and without. It is cheering you on, ready and waiting to create what it is you show you want. Don't be fooled that just because the money you desire is not in your bank account at this very moment, it is not ready for you.

Because it is, at this very moment, in existence, clearing a path for you to claim it.

The power to your magnetic vibration

Your faith and trust that these systems work all the time, without fail and want the best for you is the power to your magnetic vibration.

We vibrate in many ways at all times. We have different parts of us, and each is vibrating at a different rate. Our hair vibrates (and therefore grows) at a different rate then our liver, eyes or skin. Yet each functions constantly and replenishes itself and we benefit. Our whole BEingness is complex and vibrantly alive and active.

We have what I call systems that function together synergistically to create our physical body, and all our bodies, emotional, mental and so on. These are all vibrating differently, creating their own magnetic field as they change, transform, grow and renew. We are this amazing dance of energies blending, co creating and interacting. When you choose to incorporate all of you into your life experience, you open up so many doors. Your experience becomes multidimensional in your conscious present moment.

"I pump up my wealth vibe to maximum! I FEEL WEALTHY. I vibrate wealth. I exude wealth. Wealth is drawn to me."

If you do not think you can feel your energy, or can grasp this, think back to a time when you were upset.

When something happened you thought was bad. You got mad. What did that feel like? You felt your body change, you heart pound, your stomach churn, and you began to sweat. Energy. Why did your body react that way? You *thought.* You chose a meaning to what happened that scared, threatened or shocked you. Your thought energy, caused your brain to release certain chemicals, that created certain feelings in your body. It is all energy and it is all happening solely because you decided that event made you angry.

"I enjoy the manifestation process. I trust that my inner world is shifting my outer world, no matter what I see."

Now think about when you feel loved, appreciated, praised. You feel it in your body too. It is still just a thought that created a feeling. It is all communication. Here you see that your choices of beliefs determine how you think, feel and re-act. Communication is going on all the time, on all these levels, and all originate from thought energy.

When I met Chris, he would say he could not feel energy. He thought it was something abstract that he had not learned to tune in to yet. Then he would tell me he had a feeling about a person, or a premonition. I would say "that's energy, you are feeling it, you just have a different name for it". You are an energetic being that operates in an energetic Universe. Tune in and begin to manage your energy.

When we get all our energy and systems going in the same direction, intention wise, we are in the flow. We feel fantastic. We move through our day with ease and grace. We are internally aware and focused so we 'hear' our intuition, our inner guidance and we move with it. We do not question, second guess or allow doubt of any kind come into our awareness.

"I am inspired to create my life with ease and grace. I allow the river of wealth to carry me, gently and joyfully."

We create from within and project it without. When you are asking for more income, you tune in to it and add speed to it's manifestation by staying focused on it and *living in it mentally all the time.* This leaves no room for doubt and fear. Your dominant intent is to move INTO your vision so the income is in your physical experience of life. Your personal reality.

MAGNETIC WEALTH AFFIRMATIONS FOR YOUR WEALTH VIBE AND ENERGY

- I am in harmonious flow with the field of abundance.
- I ALIGN my wealth vibe with my vision and attract all I need to live and make it my reality.
- I exude the frequency of peace, ease, joy, love and appreciation.
- My clear imagination reveals my already existing treasure. I relax into happiness, success and creativity.
- I tune my wealth vibe and let my energy carry me easily and effortlessly.
- I tune my wealth vibe daily. I am aware of where my energy is going and what it is bringing back.
- I AM Divine creative Energy. Money is Divine creative Energy. We are one.
- I enjoy the manifestation process. I trust that my inner world is shifting my outer world, no matter what I see.
- I inspire money to flow to me. I am inspired to create my life with ease and grace.
- I allow the river of wealth to carry me, gently and joyfully.
- I Trust myself. I know the answers. I have help and I AM supported by all.
- I trust money. Money is my reliable, limitless ally. I am safe and manage money well.
- I now choose to allow my desires, intentions, thoughts and energy to align. I flow forward with ease and grace.
- I am wealthy, I feel wealthy, I carry myself like a wealthy person. Wealth feels good.

- I pump up my wealth vibe to maximum! I FEEL WEALTHY. I vibrate wealth. I exude wealth. Wealth is drawn to me.
- I Am an energetic being. I choose where my energy goes in each moment. I send my energy to what I want, and pull it back in any form that creates joy and wealth for me now.

**"ASK FOR WHAT YOU WANT. EXPECT IT. CLAIM IT.
LOOK FORWARD IN TO EACH DAY WITH AN OPEN HEART, A SENSE OF ADVENTURE...
AND A FIRM DECISION TO MAKE THIS THE MOST BLESSED, ABUNDANT AND JOYFUL DAY OF YOUR LIFE!"**

NAN AKASHA

ALIGN WITH WEALTH

Chapter 7

"Money comes from your ideas because money is just an idea."
- Robert Kiyosaki

"I used to say I don't need much. Now I don't have much."

In one of my coaching sessions on wealth transformation, this was what was written in the email from the client: "I used to say I don't need much. Now I don't have much". Can you see, just from reading it, how powerful that statement is? How it is creating her reality?!

When you say "I don't need much" or "money is not important", you are telling the universe what you want and what you are worth. You are telling yourself and your inner being is aligning with that. You are the Master...remember? You are giving the commands!

Magnetic Process:

So if you look at how you feel and what is in your life right now, physically, you can trace it back to what internal patterns and programs you were thinking and saying and living. Get your journal and make a list of what is in your life right now that you love and what is in your life that you would prefer not to have there. What you want to shift and what you want to enhance. Be clear, concise and honest. What you say has HUGE impact, on you:

1. You are programming your subconscious with repetition. If you say the same things over and over, and they do not reflect the way you really would like to feel, live and Be, then you will not manifest them. You are not lining up with the real inner you, and conflict, fear, worry occur... as well as not getting he results you want.

2. You are telling your subconscious mind, your ego, your body and all of you what you are asking for. By saying you do not need much, guess what you will get?

3. Your self worth can't align not 'needing much' with 'having a lot'. It is a disconnect.

So, look at what you say, whether you believe it or not.... especially if you are saying it to make others comfortable, be nice, agreeable or polite.

Lining up with what you choose, like more income, happiness, a new love.... has to do with INTERNAL alignment, and that includes what you say to yourself and others. What you think and say in your head too.

"I tell the universe what I want from worthiness and it responds beautifully, every time."

Be congruent: line up what you say you want (more money, peace of mind etc) with what you are saying, feeling, looking for, expecting and believing. Want it to be easier? See where you are incongruent, not lining up... saying one thing and asking for another.

"I create internal alignment. I now easily Line up with what I choose. I align with more income, more happiness, more joy and loving people."

What you have been stressing and saying you desire may be right in front of you. You cannot reach it, because you have a disconnect within your energy. Your internal and external dialogue, your vision and your feelings, your beliefs and your true sense of worth are not aligned. Therefore, not connecting. You can be one arms length from it, and literally not be able to pick it up, be blind to it!

Here is another way to think about it:

You say you want more money, you are tired of struggle and you feel that the all the things you have been doing to make it happen are not working. You explain that you have been applying for jobs, asking for raises, looking for clients, and trying to make the changes you so deeply desire happen.

You look around and say "it's the economy", "it's my prices", "it's my competitor", "it's my Dad", "it's my divorce"... it's everything outside of you. No, it's not.

"Aligning with wealth is easy! I believe my wealth is here for me. I now act, feel and speak from one mind and money flows to me daily."

It is that there are energy systems working inside you and they are not communicating. They are hearing your heart say "I want money to flow to me easily". However when the systems begin to co create what you say you choose, they encounter road blocks on the way to creating that situation.

"I shift to supportive, rich beliefs."

These road blocks are:

1. Old beliefs: like 'money is evil' then you will not get or you will get rid of money. Your inner being will not allow you to exist very long doing or having something that (you think) means you are evil.

2. Your thoughts and words: when you say you do not need much, yet are asking for a lot, there is not a way for your internal systems to rectify that. You are telling yourself two conflicting things, so you get conflicting results.

3. Doubt: if you keep going back to doubting and second guess yourself all the time, the manifestation cannot line up... it is like opening and shutting a door, it is very hard for much to get in, if you keep slamming it every few minutes!

4. Self Worth: especially when it comes to money, if your true internal compass is set at "I don't deserve" or "I am not good enough", your Money muse is cruising along, gathering resources, people, and opportunities to line you up with what you say you choose, and BAM!! A road

block! The energy of not deserving money, or whether clients will like you or you can perform well... anything like that cannot match up with the manifestation of " lots of money please".

So now your internal systems are looking around to see how they can fit that plug (more money) into that outlet (I am not good enough), because they do not match. Like a square peg in a round hole.

"I now release doubt. I pump up the volume on my self worth. I am safe, worthy and confident."

You need a converter, like when you travel, to change the voltage (your energy/frequency) and match the plug up (the meeting and melding of the desire with the reality). This is an internal shift, alignment. This is where you raise or change your vibration, the rate at which your energy is moving. You change it to match what you really want. That means shifting the belief.

If you see some results with money, but not what you really want, or you feel like you just about get money, but don't, or get it and lose it... you can be sure there are conflicting instructions going on. The alignment is internal. Not external. Don't look outside yourself for the road block. The effortless lining up happens only when the internal landscape shifts to create roads that meet and are free from blocks.

"All my bodies, systems, energy and the Universe align now for my highest good. Thank you, Thank you, Thank you."

Put yourself first, be true to what feels best for you and CHOOSE your words, thoughts and actions to be congruent with what you are asking for.

Magnetic Wealth Affirmations For Aligning with Wealth

- I tell the universe what I want from worthiness and it responds beautifully, every time.
- I am the master of my Money mind.
- I create internal alignment. I now easily Line up with what I choose. I align with more income, more happiness, more joy and loving people.
- Aligning with wealth is easy! I believe my wealth is here for me. I now act, feel and speak from one mind and money flows to me daily!
- I align my energy with my vision and all powers are on my side.
- I now release doubt. I pump up the volume on my self worth. I am safe, worthy and confident.
- I put myself first. I Am true to what feels best for me. I raise my energy to match what I truly desire.
- I shift to supportive, rich beliefs.
- I choose my words, thoughts and actions to be congruent with what I AM asking for.
- All my bodies, systems, energy and the Universe align now for my highest good. Thank you, Thank you, Thank you.

"WHAT IS YOUR RELATIONSHIP WITH MONEY? DO YOU IGNORE IT? ARE YOU ANGRY WITH IT? DO YOU THINK IT DOES NOT MATTER? ARE YOU AFRAID OF IT?

YOUR RELATIONSHIP WITH MONEY IS A KEY TO BEING WEALTHY AND INCREASING YOUR INCOME.

IF MONEY WERE A PERSON, WOULD THEY WANT TO BE AROUND YOU?"

- NAN AKASHA

Your Money Muse :
Your Relationship with Money

Chapter 8

"If you judge people, you have no time to love them." - Mother Teresa

Why do we seek wealth? Everyone does, even if they claim they don't. Wealth means comfort, happiness, no worries, and everyone wants that. We live in a world where money is required to survive and thrive. The secret is, we do not actually have to seek wealth, though. We have to **Be wealth**. It is not necessary to chase after money or success, in fact it can repel it! Instead, focusing our energy on who we are and how we feel, empowers us and we then attract an abundance of wealth.

Have you ever considered you have a relationship with money? Imagine it as a person and see how you feel about it. How you treat it. Do you blame or appreciate it? If money was your friend or lover would they want to be with you? Your attitude towards money and your relationship with money determine how much you have and how you keep, grow, share and expand it. Money is a tool, an ally, not the answer to happiness. It can enhance your life.

Money, in and of itself, is not worth seeking anyway. We all need money to live in this world, and more money does create ease and comfort. But it is not the money itself we seek, it is what money can do, buy, create and therefore fulfill for us. It is all about how we want to feel. We all want to be happy. We get to choose the meaning of all things in our life. What does money mean to you?

Magnetic Process:

In your journal define what money means to you. Ask yourself "When I think of money I feel...?" Ask "What is wealth to me now?", then ask "What do I want wealth to be/mean to me?". Look at how you treat money and feel towards money.

Sometimes, to ease our discomfort around money, switching our focus from money to what it is we really desire, opens up new doors of possibility for us. If you peel off the layers and begin to see that underneath all the pain, anger and worry over money, what you truly want is happiness, peace of mind, love, a feeling of significance.... then you can start to look to satisfy those feelings from more places.

How do you treat money?

Have you ever heard someone say "but money isn't important" or "it's not about the money"? It is interesting to me that the people who say those things make the assumption that anyone actively focused on wealth, only wants the money. What good is money just to have money? As if the money itself had any value! The money itself has no meaning, no value in and of itself. We are the ones that give money its meaning and wrap it up in emotion. But I don't believe anyone is seeking money for money. Everyone has needs and desires and they are driven by what's underneath...the joy and happiness they will feel when they get what they want. Having a passion about what you love and what meets your need for purpose, love and happiness is what fuels your focus towards wealth.

No one actually seeks wealth just to be wealthy, just to 'show off'. If it appears they do, that is insecurity and not what they truly want. They want love, and approval. Anyone who thinks it is bad to actively seek wealth has their own issues with money. I have not met one single person who does not have some issues over money and wealth. Even very wealthy ones.

The most common are fear of failure and fear of success, fear of loss and fear of being greedy or bad. Money does not mean any of these things, unless you decide to choose that meaning for it. It is unfortunate that so much anger and pain is created over the emotional meanings we give money. Money is a tool, to enhance your life. Since it is the system we use in most all societies on earth, wouldn't it be better to make friends with money? Choose positive and empowering meanings and feelings about wealth? You can't escape needing it, so make it your ally, your inspiration. It's a big step towards joy and inner peace!

Everyone may be different, but everyone wants to have a peaceful, easy, effortless relationship with money. **Everyone wants to be happy.** There is an inner knowing that tells you more money flowing to you easily and without suffering or sacrificing is a good thing and will enrich your life. Knowing you have money coming to you and you can relax and trust, gives you the energy and focus to concentrate on doing what you love. It lets you be with loved ones and create new and wonderful ideas, inventions and more. Focus on the feelings you will have when you have ease and consistency with money. These feelings are what you seek and will give you inner power. Focus on what you want, instead of the money. What you want might show up from somewhere without the need for the money. Or the money will show up from somewhere unexpected. Be open, believe you deserve it and watch with expectancy for it to show up!

"I am open and receptive to money, cash flow wealth and massive income. I ask, expect and claim my wealth now!"

Is money good or bad?

Do you want a big house? Money will get you that. Want to give to a church or charity, you need money for that. Do you want to start a business? Money will get you that too! Want to build a healing center?... money will get you that too. If you want to go on a trip, adopt a baby, have a big wedding, get a new couch, go back to school, give to a charity, get a massage every week, hire help in our business, hire a cleaning service, help your kids and friends out, rescue animals, heal your body....Money can help.

These are the things we want... and money is vital to getting them. But realize this, these things are the surface appearance of life. They are wonderful and we all deserve to have them. But the true motivator is how we will FEEL when we get them, give them, experience them.

No one wants money for money, it's pointless. People are driven by their needs, for feeling good, for having a purpose.

So, now you can let go of the guilt. You can let go feeling not good enough. You can let go of any negative thought you had about wanting to create wealth, cash flow and prosperity for yourself. Because now you know that you aren't a greedy money monger who doesn't know what is really important in life (as many people may say or think). You are a typical human, meeting your needs to feel love, joy and significance. You do know what is most important. You seek the reason for living... joy, peace, happiness, connection, love, health, sharing, giving, being your best. That is alignment. That is inner power. That will attract wealth to you. So focus on being the person you feel you will be when you have the happiness you seek, and all you need will arrive at your door in a gift box for you! Money has many surprises waiting for you!

Give yourself permission to make money!

Would you like for the wealth you have been chasing to chase you instead?

Sounds good, huh? I decided one day I would rather money came to me, than me chasing money. So I decided I want Money to run to me, play with me, stay with me. I chased Money. It doesn't work, not long term. And it isn't much fun either, right?

What, do you suppose, would make money want to look for you? What would cause wealth to shift its course and come to you? Run to you? Want to stay, play, grow and create with you? The same thing any person would want in order to desire to be with you; attention, appreciation, respect, love.

Ready to turn the flow of Money towards you and ride the wave of wealth?

Cool, me too... So I want to share with you what works and how you can get started today!

And do me a favor, will you? Don't dismiss opportunities before you have allowed your inner being to see if it is THE opportunity the Universe has lined up for you? We too often hold up the skeptic and say 'that's not for me" or "they are just selling something"... and often miss the exact opportunity we have been asking for. No matter what you feel in the moment, the Universe is always bringing you the exact opportunities to lead you to the life experience you desire.

I know everyone has some pain and frustration over Money... so wouldn't it be really great if you took this opportunity now and changed yours? Is Money flowing easily and joyfully in and out of your life?

"Money is now and always flowing easily and joyfully in my life!"

Stop fighting the flow and embody the Spirit of Money. The energy and essence of money is an energy that you can align with and attract. It is like a river of energy flowing at all times around you. I taught this in an audio. Feel the spirit of money flowing through you.

Look at your feelings about money and then reconnect with the energy and essence of Money. Understand how Money works energetically. Manage your energy and align it with money in a positive, powerful way. Learn how to magnetize yourself for receiving. This means allowing money and others to help you, you are not here to do it all alone.

When you create a new relationship with money, you need to maintain it like any other relationship you care about. Ask your money muse to appear to you and to help you, guide you, support you, and appreciate him/her in return. Ask your money muse what you should do to turn around your money situation and then do it. This is usually something fun and loving towards yourself, not something strict and boring like balance your check book.

As you do this you will release old beliefs that cause money, stress and struggle. You will feel good about money and it will begin to show up. Watch for it and celebrate it, every penny! Like you would appreciate a friend or child. Think about money as a person and how you would treat someone who had such wonderful abilities and cared for you. How would you feel towards someone you wanted in your life? How would you treat them? Now apply this towards money.

What do you believe about money? Do you believe you deserve it? Have you been told money is evil? Do you believe that wanting lots of money is greedy and selfish? This affects your attitude and feelings towards money. Your attitude towards money (or anything) creates your vibration, which will attract or repel. Are your beliefs repelling money?

Learn how to tune in to the frequency of money and trust that money will always be there for you when you want it!

"I embody the spirit of money, I am in harmonious alignment with money. Money is on my side now and always."

Alignment with money will now express into my life as:

1. money coming to me from all place, directions, expected and unexpected.

2. money flowing easily, with no emotional attachment, except gratitude/appreciation, into my life, bank account, businesses.

3. no worries in any way about money, it has no emotional reaction in me anymore, I only experience happiness/appreciation when I think of money.

4. a feeling of ease, natural, a belief that "of course money flows to me easily and effortlessly, it always does, I expect it".

5. I do what I love, what makes me happy and feel good, what my inner guidance lights up to and simply KNOW the money will flow in.

6. Money appears instantly and consistently, there is no time barrier to money, it can come instantly and it takes no special effort to attract and receive it.

7. I am always open and receptive to money, I hold the thought patterns that money loves me, I love money and we are a match. I am an excellent receiver and so money flows, grows, and glows (with energy) around and with me. I appreciate money.

8. I am friends with money, it is a natural part of my life to have more money then I need. So I bless money anytime I see or feel it, coming or going, paying or receiving. It is the flow that keeps the energy moving and energy likes movement, and money is energy.

9. I give money its respect/appreciation/attention because anything I want in my life I give attention to, in a loving, happy way.

10. money opportunities are all around me at all times, to receive it (make), to invest (grow) it, to share (give) it and to create...I see the possibilities all around me at all times.

Magnetic Process:

Change your relationship with money and magnetically attract wealth

Merge your energy field with the energy field of Money. This will help you eliminate the #1 cause of failure, stress, illness, depression, divorce; Your Relationship with Money!

Money... is it your source of Frustration or Inspiration? Decide to change that now and no longer let your inner relationship with money steal your joy and ruin your life. Believe me I have coached many people who, once they realize how angry they are with money and how disempowering their relationship with money is, see shifts in all areas of their lives. Money did not make you poor or ruin your life. No one else did either, no matter what it looks like to you. Stop being a victim and look within. *You can either be a victim or be rich, you can't be both.* Did you ever see a rich victim? Check out my "Escape the Victim Vibe" class. Very powerful way to shift.

Your relationship with money is reflected in your relationships with people in your life. If you look at your relationships, especially ones you had in childhood like with your parents or teachers, you will see how it is coloring your ability to attract money now and feel like you deserve it. Up to age seven we took on the beliefs of anyone we considered an authority. We decided what things meant from a 2, 4, or 6 year old's perspective, and those beliefs are mostly still within us! Now we get to choose our own attitude, and relationship with money, we can discard any false and unsupportive thoughts about money and create a fresh new empowering relationship.

"I am a channel for the riches of the Universe. I now allow the riches to flow to me and through me in a never ending flow."

Let's say goodbye to the inner patterns and challenges we have with wealth and worthiness. Let's consciously develop a new relationship with money that uplifts and supports us and our dreams. It is a choice, and you must make it every day, in each moment until it becomes second nature to you and automatic.

Insecurity, fear, and anxiety are holding you back from true success and ease around money. Feeling less than or not being willing to step into your power and ask for your wealth because it may offend others is self conceit, not worthiness. It is not more spiritual to not want money. It is denying your true nature. It is not letting The Universe or God express fully through you. You are denying God when you deny yourself. If you desire riches, it is God/Universe/Divine telling you that you deserve and can have them. The whole of creation is here for you. It is your playground and you have the golden key. Why not accept it?

You can see how any relationship you have is deeply affected by yourself worth, your beliefs about yourself and money and your value and worthiness. This is true for your relationship with money as well. Consciously create a relationship with money today, one that will last, is fun, reliable, mutually respectful, supportive and inspiring. Make it a relationship you get excited about. Then see how your income changes!

How would your life change if money made you feel

- Positive?
- Powerful?
- Inspired?

What would you feel if money

- Loved you!
- Ran to you!
- Played with you!
- Stayed with you!

Imagine a day where you do not worry about money... make it real in your mind. See yourself playing with, creating, sharing, giving and enjoying all money can do for you and those you love. Make it real inside you and it will appear around you.

Create a life where you can feel inner peace each day, enjoy doing what you love and have energy to enjoy your loved ones. Why not? If you think this is not possible then you are not realizing your full potential

"I Believe money loves me. I know money loves me. I know the field of abundance is a cash flow fountain.

I dip my bucket into the fountain and drink in the riches of the Divine now."

Start to take the energy and time you spent worrying, being angry, scared, frustrated and confused about money and turn it around, imagine the life you would create! Our past experiences and what we thought they meant, colors our thoughts, feelings and actions day to day. We can start right now and create a whole new relationship with money. What we have heard and been taught about money is painful, misleading and a total lie!!!

The beliefs you hold, the attitudes you have, the feelings you experience around money, income, cash, wealth and finances are in TOTAL CONTROL of your ability to allow money into your life! NOTHING you do to create income will work permanently, while you still hold inner emotions towards money that are incongruent with what you want.

You are stopping the flow of money.... you are creating the struggle! The good news is; if you created it, you can change it. Yes, YOU!

"My mind shows me the path to my wealth in every moment. I know my wealth is here. I follow my inner guidance with faith and my riches are revealed to me, now."

Is money more important than love, health or happiness? NO. Am I saying that you should worship money above all else and not care about anyone else and only care about money?

NO. If you are hearing that when you read this, you really need this!!! Money is not more important, or less important. Money is not evil, and people who have money are not inherently bad. All these false beliefs are what is ruining your financial success.

I know that at the core each living being seeks happiness and harmony. Money is a tool to help achieve that. If you could relieve your pain and anxiety around money, what kind of joy and health are you capable of experiencing?

If you did not have to spend your energy wishing you had enough money to pay bills or worrying if your next client is going to show up... what else could you use that energy for? Spending more time with your loved ones? Enjoying activities? If your mind was clear and open what ideas would be born and what riches would you discover within you?

We all want money to flow easily so we can spend our time and focus on the things we really love. Imagine the health you would have if you released your stress over money. Stress is the biggest factor in health! So increased wealth and inner ease = increased health! That increases joy, which increases love... and on it goes!

Are you starting to get it? Money is not the answer, money is your road block. Right now, money is your enemy. Is your inner voice telling you that money is hard to get? That you are greedy and unkind if you want money? How about that you are more spiritual and worthy if you do not want money? Total lies!!!

Why? Because you are born to be attuned with the flow of wellness, wonder and wealth in all areas of your life. You are meant to have and enjoy, share and give, grow and create money.

"I was born to be attuned with the flow of wellness, wonder and wealth in all areas of my life. I AM meant to have, enjoy, share, give, and grow money."

If your experience with money is negative... or like a yo - yo.. here today, gone tomorrow, look at whether you trust money. Often we do not trust ourselves, as we look to our past and say, well I didn't succeed before, or I lost it once I achieved it, so that is what I will do again. Not true!

Trust you do know how to take the next step into a higher income... or even how to add multiple income streams. Ask your money muse to help and show you the way. Develop a trusting relationship with money. Create a realizable, loving, powerful money muse to be your guide and support.

"I now have the income, cash flow and wealth I desire. I am in harmony with money. I have plenty and still more comes to me from the infinite supply. I am in alignment with infinite wealth."

Remember if you feel depressed and angry that money has been taken from you or never comes to you, let it go. No one else did it, your inner alignment and feelings about money and worthiness did. So let go of others, the past and start to create your ideal money muse now. Talk to your muse every day and begin to plan your path to wealth!

Remember you are ALREADY RICH, it is here, now, waiting for you, choose it, and let your muse help!

You may also want to look at my "Total Wealth Transformation: Meet your money muse" course. At www.MasterYourMoneyMind.com. In this course we discover our "money mask"; those beliefs and negative feelings we now have towards money. We break that relationship up and we create our "money muse". Create your money muse as your ideal relationship, one of trust, support and inspiration. Get creative and see what appears. The people in the class had amazing muses.

Here is what a few people in the course had to say:

"Nan, my money mindset has transformed so completely since working with you, that my family doesn't even recognize me!

I can't believe the difference your work has made in my life! I feel different, I am happier, more calm, and don't get caught up in the worries that my family and friends say about bills and the recession anymore!"

- Susie M. Chicago, Ill

"I was so scared and worried every day since my divorce. I thought I would not be able to pay the bills and take care of myself. When you helped me see the lies about money I was believing, it all changed! Now I have this happy, fun 'money muse' to play with and guide me and I get excited thinking about what we can create each day! Thank you from the bottom of my heart!"

                             - Marisa Rodriguez, Fla.

"The reason I am so excited about Nan's work is that since I began working with her Money Muse program, I have had $3500 of unexpected income, bonuses and freebies since December 1. Pretty impressive. Nan Akasha is the fairy Godmother of Money. I have changed my whole relationship with money and feel so connected. I feel a whole new world has opened up to me...thanks!"

    - Catherine Behan, San Diego, CA soulmatesavvy.com

"I was surprised when my money mask turned out to be a KGB agent type of sniper. It was like money was always out to get me, attack me, not to be trusted. This was so revealing.
Then when we created our money muse, mine showed up as a huge body guard/bouncer. It made me feel safe, and protected. I relaxed about money and felt I was taken care of. The relationship even developed and changed and the big body guard turned out to be a nice, sweet guy and a friend. Thank you."

                                - C. S. San Antonio, TX

"I was also stunned to see how my 'false' money appeared... it was 'greaser"/biker kind of dude, good looking, but with a real attitude, like a New Yorker guy in a leather jacket. Really manly and with that attitude of 'yeah, so what", chewing gum and slumped over in the chair. A guy who would pour attention all over you when he wanted to, and then drop you like a hot potato and not care. He was real callous and indifferent... like it was not his problem if I was not happy, too bad. I wanted to beat him up, punch and kick him and squish his face. I am a very non violent person, so this was a shock, but I went with it because I felt so safe in your class. I felt it fully, like you kept encouraging. It was a very worthless and powerless feeling. When you said to get rid of 'him', I was amazed, I kept having to do things to get rid of him, but finally he was gone and then the steel plate around my heart moved out from me and I shot it full of bullet holes (I am so anti gun you would not believe it, but this felt so good, being as it is in my mind) and it was mangled beyond repair...that felt good, because it really made me feel I could not take it back on."

-"Total Wealth Transformation: Meet Your Money Muse"
Course Participant

Money can be your friend, your ally, your protector. It is your choice. Look inside today and see how you are treating money and if you would want to be around someone who felt like that towards you.

Take yourself out of the false framework of feeling money is anything but a positive tool to enhance your life. You need money to live, and you are meant to live well, thrive and create. What I am saying is so powerful it can transform your life experience in profound ways. Meet your money muse and let it co create your wealthy life with you!

MAGNETIC WEALTH AFFIRMATIONS FOR YOUR RELATIONSHIP WITH MONEY AND YOUR MONEY MUSE

- I am open and receptive to money, cash flow wealth and massive income. I ask, expect and claim my wealth now!

- Money is now and always flowing easily and joyfully in my life!

- I embody the spirit of money, I am in harmonious alignment with money. Money is on my side now and always.

- I am a channel for the riches of the Universe. I now allow the riches to flow to me and through me in a never ending flow.

- I Believe money loves me. I know money loves me. I know the field of abundance is a cash flow fountain. I dip my bucket into the fountain and drink in the riches of the Divine now.

- My mind shows me the path to my wealth in every moment. I know my wealth is here. I follow my inner guidance with faith and my riches are revealed to me, now.

- I was born to be attuned with the flow of wellness, wonder and wealth in all areas of my life. I AM meant to have, enjoy, share, give, and grow money.

- I now have the income, cash flow and wealth I desire, I am in harmony with money. I have plenty and still more comes to me from the infinite supply. I am in alignment with infinite wealth.

**"WE ARE DIVINE WEALTHY BEINGS, HERE TO LIVE AN ABUNDANT LIFE. WE ARE MEANT TO BE WEALTHY...
IN ALL AREAS OF OUR LIFE.
ONLY WE CAN CHOOSE TO FEEL WEALTHY AND NOTICE OUR WEALTH, INVITE IN MORE AND
ACCEPT IT."**

NAN AKASHA

WHAT DOES WEALTH MEAN TO YOU?

Chapter 9

"It takes a lot of courage to release the familiar and seemingly secure, to embrace the new. But there is no real security in what is no longer meaningful. There is more security in the adventurous and exciting, for in movement there is life, and in change there is power." — Alan Cohen

Wealth to me is money, yes, and so much more! We each get to define what wealth is to us. Our natural state is wealth. When we perceive there is no wealth in our lives, it is because we are not clear on what it is and who we are.

"Wealth is a harmonious feeling, filled with fun, joy, inner peace and satisfaction. I am fulfilled in every way as I allow myself to live and enjoy my wealthy life."

We are divine wealthy beings, here to live an abundant life. We are meant to be wealthy... in all areas of our life. Only we can choose to feel wealthy and notice our wealth, invite in more and accept it. If you are not experiencing wealth in your life, you do not feel you deserve it. You are not aware of it, or looking for it.

Magnetic Process:

First you must define what wealth means to you. It is more than money, yet it most definitely includes money. Wealth includes a harmonious combination of all things you love and enjoy. Wealth is money, cash flow, income, investments, that come to you from multiple places and that you receive openly. Wealth is unexpected income, surprise gifts, coupons, discounts, deals and loans. Wealth is all forms of riches, like gold, silver, stocks and any other form of valuable item, even your house and paintings, art and things like stamp collections, that have value.

Wealth is love, joy, happiness, health, energy, clarity, focus. Wealth is friends and loved ones, adventurous experiences, opportunities for any and everything you decide you love. If you love to travel, and you receive a trip or an opportunity to go somewhere you love, that is wealth. If you want to do something and someone invites you to do it and pays for it, that is wealth. Wealth is receiving and giving gifts, compliments, love, caring and appreciation.

"I open to receive the prosperous gifts the Universe has for me now. I love receiving gifts. I awake each day in joyful anticipation of the prosperous surprises waiting for me!"

Wealth is a feeling, a state of mind. Wealth is the feeling of inner peace that your day is unfolding just as it should. It is feeling good and people who are kind and helpful. Wealth is getting more or better than you expected. Wealth is even spending time enjoying your home and the things you have, the wonderful memories and people in your life. Wealth is you. Wealth is life-force, being alive, here and now. Wealth is all things that uplift, delight, empower and touch and inspire you.

"I love how I always receive more than I ask for. I expect to be provided for lavishly and enjoy the flow."

Wealth is an energy of love, expectation, appreciation and enjoyment. Fulfillment, satisfaction and inner peace. Wealth is your divine right, your natural state and it is only when you do not see it, feel worthy of it and open yourself to fully receive it, that you live in a state of 'poverty'. Poverty is also a state of mind, a feeling and an attitude. Choose wealth, it is who you truly are.

"I feel the vibration of love flowing through me. I feel gratitude for all I have. I feel a part of the abundance of the universe now."

Wealth is a healthy, flexible, energetic body that gets younger each day. Wealth is the feeling of cozy comfort.

Wealth is your natural state. You do not have to do anything to be worthy of wealth. You are worthy of wealth exactly as you are right now. You do not have to be anything anyone else thinks you need to be to have wealth. When you are BE-ing yourself wealth flows to you. You allow wealth into your life experience when you are fully merged with your true nature. Wealth flows to you... receive it with appreciation and joy. Celebrate the wealth you have, the wealth that is coming to you, the wealth that is you.

"I am worthy of wealth just being myself. Wealth flows to me and I receive it with appreciation and joy. I celebrate the wealth I have, and the wealth that is coming to me. I see it, feel it, claim it, now."

Top 3 impacts your feelings about money has on you

You will be shocked at how big an impact money has on your life. In the chapter on your money muse I shared some of the experiences my total wealth transformation class had. I, personally, already know how huge the impact our feelings and beliefs about money have on our health, happiness and life. I have experienced wealth and poverty, joy and sadness, loss and abundance. I know that the key to life is joy. I know that when we are happy, we align with all things good, and our life flows. I know that money is a huge stressor, and stress causes illness, depression and divorce. Happiness relieves stress and so much more.

So what does that have to do with money? Well, if you look at your relationship with money, and your experience with money, you will easily see the in congruency. Money, in our society, is a necessity and is highly emotionally charged and sought after. We all had experiences in childhood that made us feel powerless, it is the nature of being a child. Your parents were in control of almost everything, especially money. Their attitudes, emotions and patterns about money were the first experience you had with it. That started you placing meaning and emotions onto money. You wanted something and if you got it you felt happy. If your parents said no, or 'I can't afford it", or "do I look like I am made of money", and you did not get it, you felt sad, angry or frustrated. Human nature. You naturally want to be happy.

Well, it is really no different as an adult. We have things we want, from a nice house or car to the ability to put our kids through college, leave a foundation for charity or take a trip. Whatever it is you want, you want it because you think it will make you happy, make you feel good. Most of the things you want, require money. Even the feeling of security, safety and peace of mind that you can pay your bills, require money. So you can see, there is no way you can avoid money having an impact on your life. Add to that the emotions attached to having money or not, and you begin to see how you rarely go through a day without some kind of money experience touching you. The thing is, most adults have not taken any time to look at how they feel about money, or 'work on' their relationship with money. Most people do not even realize that they do have a relationship with money, and most likely it is negative, and energy draining.

Impact #1: **Health**. We all know what stress does to our health and if you experience it severely enough, severe dis-ease. If you are worried about money or your job, angry with an ex or boss about money, you have money stress. If you feel not good enough or worthy or even have a lot of money and worry about losing it, you have money stress. Your inner peace and happiness are directly related to how you feel about money and that is directly related to your energy, focus, clarity, creativity, flexibility, and body image.

Impact#2: **Divorce**. Even if you are not married, any relationship, especially love ones, suffer greatly due to disagreements over money. Money is the proven #1 cause of divorce and break up. Imagine, someone you love more than anyone else in the world, and you have such strong, negative feelings about money, you let it ruin your primary relationship. Don't believe me? Look at you and your spouse, or partner's ideas and attitudes about money. They will be aligned to some degree, but everyone carries their old baggage. Your upbringing and beliefs about money are not the same. You have different levels of desire for things, and therefore prioritize them differently. As your relationship changes and grows, so do you, and you will see your limiting beliefs about money create conflict.

Impact #3: **Failure**. What I mean by failure is several things. Failure to do what you really want and follow your heart. Failure to ask for what you want, because you fear rejection. Failure to value yourself enough, that others see your worth and pay you well. Failure to start or complete. Failure to love yourself enough to put your feelings first so you have more to give others. Failure to believe in yourself. Failure to share your ideas, love, energy and uniqueness. Failure is a state of being, feeling like a failure for a multitude of reasons. Worried about being a failure, keeping you from acting on ideas that would bring wealth, love and joy.

Feeling like a failure, or fearing failing, is hugely tied to money. Most people value themselves based on income, job title, success in monetary terms. Most people want more money yet experience fear of failure that keeps them from trying to create more. If you feel like a failure because you do not make enough money, or you made money and lost it, or you fear losing it, or are afraid to start a business because you might fail, money is impacting your life big time!

"Wealth means ease, and abundance with money. Consistent cash flow. Doing what I love. Wealth is serving others by being me and sharing my unique and special talents."

So, how do you loosen and release the amount of impact money has on you and your life?

So now you know how big an impact your feelings, beliefs and patterns around money have on your life. One of my classes "Total Wealth Transformation: Meet Your Money Muse" had all kinds of transformative realizations in just the first class! Here are just a few of the many comments and feedback. I have lots of class participants who are noticing resistance, and fears coming up, and already seeing them shift! This is wonderful! Awareness is the key to open the door to your freedom and flow with money.

"I loved the meditation tonight! It was the first time I "felt" the *material* wealth all around me. I've felt webs of energetic abundance before, but this time I was moving around the city noticing all of the physical luxury and wealth kinesthetically. This happened quite spontaneously and took me rather by surprise. Your meditations are absolutely wonderful!

And your energy is so clear and conscious." - Wanda P

"I felt really good immediately after the first class. The very next day after your first Wealth class, I got a new client from out of the blue who started right away and paid me $500... plus a new affiliate. Your processes make me feel so positive and open. Thank you" - CS

Want to see the impact your false relationship with money is creating? See what these students are realizing and releasing:

"SO SO hard for me to keep my mind straight. I feel pressure all the time to get to ground zero... it is hard for me to trust my inner voices."

"Each time I get ready to set a coaching session with you, I feel resistance. I realize I am afraid to find out what it is that is holding me back."

"During the first meditation I felt like a box of steel was around my heart. I felt almost paralyzed to take action. It was so obvious to me that I had believed what 3 specific people in my life had made me feel ; "I don't deserve" and that without them I was nothing. I have been living inside a box that told me my success and the money I had or could get, was all based on what they decided for me. It was so frustrating to see that I have limited myself based on the belief I have held since early childhood: that others are in control of the money and abundance and I have to please them in order to be 'good enough' to be allowed to receive some of it. And that when I did receive it, I had to be good or they would take it away or not give me anymore."

"I also felt like I was watching this from a distance and that part of me really noticed how just that was enough of a 'stuck' energy, to keep me from consistently flowing with money. I am good at creating money and chunks of it. I want it to flow all the time and not feel like I always have to prove myself and wait on someone else's approval to get what I want. I want to feel free! When you took us into the field of abundance it started to ease and I felt supported all around. I truly felt like this past block is gone, now I have to find a new way to feel and act.... so interested to see what is next. Thank you... this process is already worth it ten times over!"

"every time I start to plan (my business) ....I stop...after seemingly wasting all the time and money on my other business building plan, I am flat out afraid to walk in a new direction... and when it comes to creating a fee schedule for myself (both personal service and workshops) I freeze..."

Do you relate to any of this? Can you see how powerful your ideas, feelings and relationship with money is? It starts with self worth and radiates out from there. I know you are ready to transform these kinds of feelings into the breakthroughs and empowering new thoughts that bring inner peace, happiness and cash flow. Now is your chance, ride this wave of transformation! Master Your Money Mind now!

"Wealth is my state of mind. Wealth is having my money muse as my ally, inspiration and guide."

"So....you are not going to believe this but..... I got a five hundred dollar check in the mail today....a reimbursement for a hospital bill from when I was sick. I also had a great conversation with one of my brothers (hadn't heard from him in a long time) I needed some new shirts and found the perfect ones, the perfect colors and priced two for one.

I am really seeing that abundance IS more than money!! Larry also got a 75 dollar check for an overpayment... you ARE the fairy godmother!!

I mean it though about your magic. It is amazing that I get such tangible results with you...I do hope you make a monthly offering so people like me can support you and be in your vortex!" - Catherine Behan, San Diego CA

"I'm learning a lot and noticing how big an impact money has on my life and on others in my life and how often I think about it. WOW!" - Sandy Meredith

Thank you to all who share their breakthroughs, to all who attend my classes and buy my products. You are a blessing to me, I love to uncover this interesting journey with you!

"Wealth is love, loving myself brings me more wealth. It is the gateway to true wealth and happiness. Wealth is being loved by others and enjoying my lovability."

Be Happier; Make More Money

If you know me, you know I am big on being joyful, having fun, feeling good. Changing how you feel, changes everything. It sounds simple, but it is true. It is what we all want anyway. Happiness. So why don't more people get that? It sounds too simple to be true People often ask me the single most important thing they can do to achieve success. I would quote a wonderful song "Don't Worry, Be Happy now". Happiness is always the bottom line.

If you really do want to relieve your stress over the 'recession' and open the door to more wealth, no matter what is going on around you, focus on feeling good, be happy.

Magnetic Process:

Make way for wealth and riches to flow into your life even in a recession, by deciding to be happy and look for the good in your life. Start a PROOF JOURNAL (also called a gratitude journal). Every night look back over your day and write the things that went well for you, even if it was only finding a penny on the road. Search for them. Then feel very grateful for it. As you do this you will:

- build proof that good things do happen to you.
- see when you ask for money it begins to come and things happen.
- you can go back and read this when you get down to motivate you.
- you train your mind to look for the good and therefore attract more good!

"I choose wealth. It is who I truly AM. Wealth chooses me. We are one and any separation is an illusion. I know I am one with wealth now and always."

People who are happy earn $750,000+ more in their lifetime than others. More than 255 studies show that money doesn't buy happiness. Studies say it is the other way around: Happiness brings money.

Happy people are more open minded, relaxed, and that focus of positive energy brings more inner peace. Even in challenging times. This creates more in the moment awareness which makes them able to see that everything is opportunity. Therefore they have more opportunities. Cultivate a happy attitude, you will then get to enjoy life more and definitely attract more goodies! Money loves happy vibes!

MAGNETIC WEALTH AFFIRMATIONS FOR ALIGNING WITH WEALTH

- I open to receive the prosperous gifts the Universe has for me now. I love receiving gifts. I awake each day in joyful anticipation of the prosperous surprises waiting for me!
- I love how I always receive more than I ask for. I expect to be provided for lavishly and enjoy the flow.
- I inspire money to flow to me. I am inspired to create my life with ease and grace. I allow the river of wealth to carry me, gently and joyfully.
- I feel the vibration of love flowing through me. I feel gratitude for all I have. I feel a part of the abundance of the universe now.
- Wealth means ease, and abundance with money. Consistent cash flow. Doing what I love. Wealth is serving others by being me and sharing my unique and special talents.
- Wealth is my state of mind. Wealth is having my money muse as my ally, inspiration and guide.
- Wealth is a harmonious feeling, filled with fun, joy, inner peace and satisfaction. I am fulfilled in every way as I allow myself to live and enjoy my wealthy life.
- I choose wealth. It is who I truly AM. Wealth chooses me. We are one and any separation is an illusion. I know I am one with wealth now and always.
- Wealth is love, loving myself brings me more wealth. It is the gateway to true wealth and

happiness. Wealth is being loved by others and enjoying my lovability.

- I am worthy of wealth just being myself. Wealth flows to me and I receive it with appreciation and joy. I celebrate the wealth I have, and the wealth that is coming to me. I see it, feel it, claim it, now.
- Wealth is my state of mind. Wealth is having my money muse as my ally, inspiration and guide.
- Wealth is love, loving myself brings me more wealth. It is the gateway to true wealth and happiness. Wealth is being loved by others and enjoying my lovability.
- I choose wealth. It is who I truly AM. Wealth chooses me. We are one and any separation is an illusion. I know I am one with wealth now and always.

"YOUR MIND IS THE GATEWAY TO REALITY.
IT IS YOUR FILTER AND YOUR ASSISTANT.

YOUR MIND SOLVES PROBLEMS FOR YOU
BASED ON WHAT YOU CHOOSE TO BELIEVE.
WHAT ARE YOU SEEING, AND BELIEVING?"

- NAN AKASHA

Install a wealthy mindset

Chapter 10

"If you think you can, you can. And if you think you can't, you're right." - Henry Ford

We now understand how powerful our mind is. We have many levels working at the same time. What we can do to powerfully change our lives, is to be aware that our mindset is vital to having, being and doing what we truly desire.

Magnetic Process:

You can install a powerful mindset through the following process. We do not need to go into our entire story about what has happened to us in the past, or why. You need to know and choose these three things:

1. I AM the master Creator of my reality, and I can choose anything NEW right now.
2. What I repeat, with passion, my mind and the Universe will hear and act on.
3. My 'job' is to be clear and congruent with myself and others on who I AM, what I claim and stay aware in the moment to see it appearing and take action.

If you want to cleanse, clear and release all the thoughts, beliefs and thought patterns that no longer support you in creating, attracting and receiving wealth, this is for you! All you need is to be ready, willing, open and receptive and you are on your way!

Magnetic Process:

So start by opening your energy field, feel good and relax. Let all your muscles, mind and energy relax and open. Create a safe space and suspend your disbelief. Now repeat and FEEL each of the following statements. Allow them to move through you, feeling how you react in your body, mind and emotions. Keep choosing this as your reality.

The most powerful way to install this is to listen or repeat it daily for 32 days. Feel it powerfully and enhance the vision each time.

"I am wealthy. I have a wealthy mind. I have a wealthy mindset.

My mind knows to find the opportunities that bring wealth to me through ease, joy and love.

I AM fully aware and present in the moment to embrace those opportunities, to see and know and feel those opportunities.

I take a step forward fully trusting and knowing that I AM deserving, I AM beautiful, that I have so much to offer.

I am a wealthy being. I AM a wealthy _____ (woman, man, business person, mother...).

I AM wealthy now and here.

I claim my wealth. I state myself as a wealthy Person of the Universe.

I AM a wealthy citizen of a wealthy global community, on a wealthy world, in a wealthy Universe. Wealth is everywhere. Wealth is everywhere I look. There is more than enough wealth for everyone.

My desire, my ability and my willingness to open to, claim and receive my wealth now, expands the ability for all others to do the same.

I can help more people by being wealthy myself and embracing my own natural wealthy vibration, then by anything else that I do.

So I claim that now, for myself and for everyone.

I AM wealthy."

You may get a free mp3 audio of this in a one hour healing by going to http://tinyurl.com/yzll2vq

This is from my free Intend Global Healing calls. We cleansed our minds and the global mind and installed a wealthy mindset.

To hear about all the free healings go to www.IntendGlobalHealing.com

"WE ARE MAGNETIC BEINGS. WE ATTRACT
EVERY SINGLE THING IN OUR LIVES, FROM
OUR MONEY TO OUR RELATIONSHIPS, TO
OUR FEELINGS BASED ON THE QUALITY AND
DIRECTION OF OUR VIBRATION.
READY TO TAKE BACK YOUR LIFE?

YOU HAVE THE POWER WITHIN YOU TO
DIRECT YOUR ENERGY AND MANIFEST
ANYTHING YOU DESIRE WITH EASE AND
GRACE."

- NAN AKASHA

YOU ARE ALREADY RICH!

Chapter 11

"One of the tragic things I know about human nature is that all of us tend to put off living. We are all dreaming of some magical rose garden over the horizon -
instead of enjoying the roses that are blooming outside our windows today."   -
Dale Carnegie

In the present moment we have the power to change, to be aware, to choose what we want and to allow our desires to appear.

Yes, I said appear. Since all is energy and all possibilities exist in each moment, there is nothing kept from you, nothing you have to create and chase and take. You only need to align with your wealth, and it will appear to you. It is, in fact already here, right now. Your riches, your joy, your health are all here, right now. Why don't you see them, feel them? You are looking at something else. You don't expect it to appear. You are too focused on what you don't have.

Magnetic Process:

What are you looking at? What are you experiencing? (Take a moment and write those questions down. Contemplate it and notice that whatever is prominent in your life is what you spend the most time on). If it is not what you really want, decide to look for something else. It is there. You are the only one who is preventing yourself from seeing and having the wealth. We need not worry about making anything happen, only shift our inner perspective. Then we will see things as opportunities that did not seem like opportunities before. We will notice we are drawn to certain people, we want to go to certain places. When you begin to align with your true wealthy nature, love yourself and watch where your energy and focus are going, you will see things you thought did not exist before!

Magnetic Process:

Take a moment and write down: "What opportunities exist, right now, in my life?" and then list them, look for them meditate on it and see what comes up. I can guarantee you that something, probably many things, you have been asking for, are already in your life, and you just have not noticed it, not seen it as an opportunity. You may know it is an opportunity but are afraid to do it. Once you find one or a few, now ask yourself "How do I take advantage of this opportunity the Universe has brought to me?"... see what comes. Finally, make a commitment to yourself that you will take action on at least one of these opportunities today!

Keep in mind, what you want is ALREADY HERE! Your wealth, riches, money, income… it's already here, waiting for you to tune your inner wealth vibe to it. Your job is to align with it, BE it, choose to deserve it so you can see and enjoy it!

"All Possibilities Exist right Now. My good, my wealth and my ideal life exist right now. I tune in to them and allow them to appear. I am safe, free and powerful."

You see, all possibilities exist in this moment, In every moment. What does this mean for you and I? It means that we can tune in to, or become aware of any one of those possibilities. We can even choose the one we want. If you are struggling with money, then decide you want to BE the wealthy you, you now choose to align with, find, unveil, uncover, let out… the rich you.

Once we are aware of what we want and tune in to it, it comes into focus. Like focusing a microscope. We do not see it unless we are aware we want it. Then we begin to think about it, thus telling our mind and the field of abundance that this is important to us. The more we think about it, the more we begin to see it, hear about it, learn about it. We are attracting it.

Decide right now to believe that in this and each moment you can focus on and choose whatever it is you want to be true for you. *It is already in existence, it does not have to be made, it simply has to be found by internal, vibrational alignment*. When we find it within us, we align with it outside of us. This is manifestation. This is when you step into the experience of wealth. The wealth is always there. You just have not 'seen' it, matched up to it. It is ALREADY THERE. You are ALREADY RICH. Now it is time to uncover it and live in it.

In order to attract money, wealth or anything else, we must first make it a priority. Our mind listens to what we repeat the most often with the most passion. It is solving the problem, attracting the resources and anything else that must happen in order for you to have the riches you are asking for. We must accept that the money:

- Exists right now, whether we see it or not
- We can tune in to it and 'uncover' it.
- We deserve it.
- It is ALREADY THERE!
- We are Already rich, despite what we see and experience in this moment.
- The wealth does not have to come from, or be taken form, anyone else.

When we accept that all possibilities exist in every moment, we choose to believe that it is already in existence. Then we know all we have to do is locate it and claim it.

Magnetic Process:

Relax and close your eyes, make sure you are somewhere you can be quiet and uninterrupted.

Imagine you are deep within yourself, all the way to the core. There is a secret door. You see the door, it is huge, decorated and ornate. You go to open it, and it slides open at the touch of your finger.

As you enter this deep, inner chamber of "you", you smell the most wonderful fragrances, you hear soft sounds of waves, breezes and other relaxing sounds. You feel 'at home' and relax more deeply.

In here, your true self resides. All the parts of you that you are afraid of, or feel you need to hide from others. Even the parts that you are scared to express because you do not feel good enough.

You are here to see what you ALREADY have. What you ALREADY are and what you can ALREADY do. Go on a treasure hunt, look around, explore the rooms, the halls, the closets. Find the true essence of you, find the wealthy you!

Here you are looking for the wealthy you, and see what that looks like, feels like and see it is a reality. Since all possibilities exist in this and each moment, the rich, happy, healthy you exists right now. I want you to find it and play with it. Step into it and see how it feels. Make it real, and then decide to let it out of this room. Bring it with you and begin, daily, to step into the wealthy you.

Choose the possibility you like, and make it your reality!

Repeat until you feel it with all of you, easily! Enjoy!

MAGNETIC WEALTH AFFIRMATIONS FOR BEING ALREADY RICH!

- All Possibilities Exist right Now. My good, my wealth and my ideal life exist right now. I tune in to them and allow them to appear. I am safe, free and powerful.

- I choose to BE the wealthy me. I know there are infinite versions of me, and I choose the wealthy, healthy happy one, now!

- I decide right now to believe that in this and each moment I focus on and choose what I desire and it is true for me.

- I now step into the experience of wealth. The wealth is always there, and I choose to live it now.

- I have the power to change, to be aware, to choose what I want and I allow my desires to appear.

- I shift my inner perspective and see opportunities all around me. I am an opportunity magnet.

- I choose the possibility I like, and make it my reality!

"TRUE CHANGE MUST BEGIN WITHIN. IF YOU DO NOT SET YOUR INTENTIONS FIRMLY INTO YOUR ENERGY AND GIVE YOUR MIND AND THE UNIVERSE A CLEAR VISION OF WHAT YOU TRULY WANT, *NOTHING YOU DO WILL WORK FOR LONG.***"**

- NAN AKASHA

Reboot Your Inner Money Machine

Chapter 12

"Limitless riches are flowing to me as fast as I can receive and use them, and every man gets richer day by day." - Joseph Murphy

I encourage clients to listen to my guided meditations, activations and hypnosis audios on a regular basis. Why? Because as a Master level Hypnotherapist I have seen amazing transformations in people, their mindset, their inner peace and their level of faith when they commit to repetition. You can program your mind and create automatic ways of thinking and being that attract, receive and grow wealth.

I want to share a breakthrough story from a client who used my audio "Reboot Your Inner Money Machine" (available at createyourownrealitynow.com). This client who was in my classes and was using the 'Reboot your Inner Money Machine 'audio daily had a most amazing breakthrough. Because she was internally committed to make changes to her income, and relationship to Money she listened diligently to the audio each day. As her Money attitudes and energy began to shift, her limiting beliefs and emotions around Money began to loosen up, shift and rise to the surface. This is good, although often a bit of an uncomfortable feeling.

One day she was restless and annoyed as she listened. As this is a meditation, relaxation audio, you must sit or lay down and listen and follow along. The more she listened, the more irritated she became. So she decided to get up and do the dishes and continue to listen to the audio that way. While this is highly unusual, being a meditative audio, she was dedicated to her transformation.

As she did dishes and listened, she suddenly had a massive breakthrough! She was overwhelmed with the realization that she was filled with anger. Anger towards Money! A flood of understanding poured through her. She was angry with Money because it meant her husband had to go to work for long hours to make ends meet and she was not able to be with him as much as she liked. She was angry with Money because she could not buy her kids the things they desired. She was angry with Money because the fact that she needed it to live, meant she and her family could not do what they wanted.

When you uncover these deep hidden beliefs and emotions around Money, you can shift your relationship with Money! You are now able to see how your feelings towards Money deeply affect how you feel, what you attract and how you live! Now, you can make some truly transformational shifts in your energy and attract more wealth with joy!

Share your breakthroughs and breakdowns with me! Let me know how else I can help you Free your mind and let the wealth follow!

Here is a description of the Reboot Your Inner Money Machine audio. It was a spontaneous vision and activation that occurred to me during one of my daily meditations. It was so powerful I redid it and then recorded it to share.

This powerful Audio Activation opens the floodgates to your worthiness and your wealth. Become infused with magnetic energies. "An avalanche of unserving money beliefs fall away, your heart opens and you vibrate with the frequency of money". You are activated to magnetically draw money to you in an ever increasing speed and flow. Hear the voice of money, merge with the Spirit of Money. Become a money machine. This 30 minute guided meditation takes you to a deep state of relaxation where you can access your limiting beliefs and transform them into positive, money attracting ones. It will bring you a sense of calm as well as allow your limiting emotions to come to the surface, where you can then identify them and let them go.

This is my most popular audio, and it is because it is more than a meditation, it is an activation, a remembering on a cellular level of your value and worthiness. In the vision you actually began to produce money from within you and send it out into the world. Then it begins to come back to you. Think about this for a minute. We tend to think of money and wealth being something that is outside of us. That we have to go get, earn, hunt it down. Imagine how powerful it would be if you switched that perspective and began to see yourself as a money machine, the money and wealth coming from within you! This is closer to the energetic truth anyway!

So reboot your inner money machine today, begin to feel money and wealth within you and send it out into the world to find more and bring it back to you!

Here are a few of the comments from users of the 'Reboot Your Inner Money Machine' audio.

"This recording is absolutely incredible. The changes I feel are amazing. I cannot explain the gratitude I have for you sharing this. Amazing!"   - Jeremy

"I really appreciate the Reboot Your Inner Money Machine activation. I am doing it every day and each time it is more fun and powerful. I love the feeling of being merged with the Spirit Of Money and how wonderful it is to be aware of that alignment throughout my day...fabulous. I love where I am at and am excited for what is coming next."

"Hi Nan, I am having great fun with the 'Reboot Your Inner Money Machine', every time I use it is different and I never know what to expect! Thanks for sharing your wisdom. You give great answers that feel positive and empowering. Love & Gratitude..."

That's just a few of MANY that are releasing their limiting beliefs and tuning in to the flow of money! Be in the "flow" with the energy of wealth cash, riches....

"IMAGINE LIVING THIS YEAR BEING YOUR
IDEAL INCOME, BODY, HEALTH, FRIENDS,
JOB, BUSINESS.
IMAGINE REALLY MAKING THE CHANGES, IN
A NATURAL, COMFORTABLE, FUN WAY.
IMAGINE BEING NATURALLY MOTIVATED,
INSPIRED AND MAGNETIC."

- NAN AKASHA

Your Wealth Image

Chapter 13

*"Our self-image and our habits tend to go together.
Change one and you will automatically change the
other."*
- Dr. Maxwell Maltz

I told you I like to go to the core, to get the fastest and most accurate results. The core of who you are is your Self image. Your Self image is the blueprint from which your systems operate. It is what your mind, your ego, and the Universe use as a guide to know what you want. Remember these systems are here 24/7 working to bring you what you want.

"Why don't I have the money I want then?" You ask. I'll bet a large portion of you reading this book right now, have read tons of books, taken classes and tried meditating, visualizing, making vision boards and more, with some or no results.

It's not that these techniques aren't useful. It is that you can only make 'skin deep' changes when you do not first change your Self image. It is a bit like covering up an ugly old chair with a blanket. It may look better, but it is still an ugly old chair underneath. It will never change by covering it with hopes, wishes and weak affirmations.

Will power works only when applied to keeping focused on your vision and staying committed to your goal. It is not to be used to change habits, beliefs or create true transformation. Anyone who has ever been on a diet knows this. What always happens in the end? You cannot sustain the diet because it is not transforming you from within. It is attempting to force a change on you from outside.

Your shift must occur within you first, in order to transform your outer world experience. Change the internal landscape, energy and image, and the outside naturally shifts to match. It can literally dissolve and then take the shape of your new self image in an instant, if you let it!

"I now shift my energy to fun and empowering feelings. I choose my life on purpose. I transform through awareness and choice."

Have you ever had the experience of deciding to let something go in your mind and you feel different immediately? Or to intentionally change how you feel about something or someone? What happens? Instantly you experience things in a new way. Learning to shift your energy and thus your emotions is fun and empowering. When you are able to do this on demand, you are choosing your life on purpose. This is what transforming from within is all about. It did not take effort, struggle, a long time and a lot of stress and deprivation. It did not take will power. It only took awareness and choice.

So to create lasting change and permanent wealth you first start with your WEALTH IMAGE.

What is your wealth image? In the chapter "Already Rich", we did a magnetic process where you went to the secret room within you and looked for the wealthy you. This is a great start on seeing your current self and wealth image, and beginning to change it to what you prefer. It is your internal, self image in terms of wealth, money, income, and the worthiness you feel towards it. Your Self image is how you see, think of and feel about yourself. It is not a reflection of your true self. Your true self is divine, abundant wealthy, healthy, living, happy and limitless in all ways, always.

"I am connected to my true wealth image and the Universe supports me in every moment."

Your Self image was formed when you were growing up, We are in theta brain state till we are about 7. This means we are wide open, absorb easily, and take on almost anything that is presented from an authority or with emotions. So you in fact now believe things about yourself that are untrue. You believe things about yourself that a 1, 2, 5, 7, year old decided. No wonder you don't feel good and aligned with yourself! You would not let a 2 or 5 year old decide for you now. You know that a child has only certain conscious understanding. You know that things you thought were great and real as a child are not your reality anymore.

So it is time to revamp your Self image and your wealth image. It is time to transform from within. This is fun!

Magnetic Process:

Creating Your New Wealth Image

"Striving for real success - for your success - through creative accomplishment, brings a deep inner satisfaction. Striving for a phony success to please others brings a phony satisfaction."
- Dr. Maxwell Maltz

In order to attract, create, receive and enjoy wealth, you must see yourself as wealthy. You must believe you are wealthy. You must feel what it is like to be wealthy in just the way you desire. Not what others think. It must come from within you as a sincere desire. Remember, to manifest in physical reality, we must live in it mentally first.

Desire is the Divine source energy moving through you... communicating to you! Desire is the Universe telling you, 'this is what you want, it will thrill you, expand you, give you what you most need". It means it is the right thing for you at the time. It means you have the means, strength, vision and courage to make it happen, It means the Universe is on your side.

What you Believe is True for You and Nothing Else

Your Self image and wealth image are the controlling blueprint you have created consciously or unconsciously.

It must be changed by conscious intent in order for you to alter your life experience and to attract and keep wealth. Your energy field is always moving and interacting with everyone and everything around you. It is a projection of your Self image and your thoughts and feelings about yourself and what you believe. Self esteem or what I call "wealth esteem" is a potent part of your wealth vibe... the vibration you put out that causes law of attraction to respond and bring you what you currently have. And this is the core. This is where I like to go.

"I allow the unsupportive patterns to dissolve and then take the shape of my new Wealth self image in an instant. I let it go, now."

In order to create your reality the way you truly want it you must discover a few things. Get your wealth journal or start one about your new wealth image and write this down and answer it, clearly and in short phrases.

1. What you want.
2. Why you want it.
3. When you want it.
4. How much you want.
5. What it will feel like to have/BE/do it.

There are many tools that help with manifesting. Being conscious, aware and open.

To create with mastery is to:

- own your power.
- to accept your worthiness.

- ask with clarity.

"I claim my power. I step into my power. I know my power is Divine, safe and for my highest good."

Are you making positive changes in your life and feeling uncomfortable around people you once were uplifted by? Your wealth image must be one you choose from within. It cannot be what you think others want from you. Once you start to transform from within, realize others around you may not be.

Are you on a path of personal growth and really making changes? Are you feeling more happy, empowered, positive and in charge of your life? Great! That is my passion, to help anyone who seeks a better life and more joy, love, wealth and health to find it within themselves and create the life they desire! This is what we all seek, even if some people are so buried in their fear and pain they can't see a way out. My total wealth transformation class has seen amazing inner shifts in the way they feel, how they see the world and what they are choosing. The results are fantastic. Now, the changes are becoming more real and they are beginning to see others in their environment react to their positive changes.

Whenever we make changes that empower us, in how we feel and what we create, those who know us as we have been will react. If you are fortunate enough to have truly supportive, open minded and growth seeking people in your life, you will be supported. However, most of us soon experience many people around us reacting negatively. This is their issue, not ours, and yet we have to address it within us. You will find that you will shift who you are hanging out with and what you want. You will see certain relationships fade and people move away from you and others appear. It is natural. In essence you have raised your vibration as well as your awareness.

Allow the people in your life to move out and in as you change your Wealth Image

I have been through this many times, because I am on a constant, intense path of inner growth and change. I strongly desire to be personally empowered, joyful, wealthy and happy all the time. The more I did this, the more I found I just could not be around certain people and in certain groups. At first it can be hard. I remember about 10 years ago I was mostly a stay at home mom and had these wonderful women friends and women's spiritual groups I attended. They were my lifeline to sanity and they were very nurturing. It really felt so wonderful to be with them. We would meet several times a month, go on retreats and so on. I loved being with them and doing all the meaningful activities which included spiritual and personal growth work, which I love.

"I now allow my inner brilliance to shine. I unleash my radiance.
I embrace my luster.
I am radiant, joyful and prosperous.
I love expressing myself fully.
This or something better.
Thank you Thank you Thank you"

I was tired from being with twin babies all the time and still had some deep sadness I had not fully released from my daughter dying several years before. In this space with these women, I was taken care of and it felt so good, because I was depleted of energy taking care of others all the time. At that time, they were a perfect match for me, and I gained so much by being with them. They enjoyed caring for women who were needy and I had needs. It worked well and uplifted me for years.

"I am safe and loved. The Universe
is on my side.
I have the strength, smarts and courage to handle
anything that comes my way.
I am supported and follow my inner guidance
without hesitation."

Then I began to find more inner joy and met one woman in particular. We became friends and she was fun, strong, and opinionated and did her own thing. She came to the groups now and then, but really had her own way of doing things. I began to feel more joyful, and strong and clear. I began to do more healing work again and as my kids approached school age, I felt ready to grow a business again. I spent more time with her and less with the group. She made me feel strong and empowered. The group did not like my new found energy, happiness and strength. They separated us in groups so we did not act too happy and outgoing. They commented that when I spent time with her I was "too energetic" and yes, believe it or not "too happy"! I began to feel less supported by the group and even found myself 'seeing' things about them I didn't notice before. They were very focused on weakness and wounds. They liked new people who joined the group and were weak and needy, like I had been years before. They had severe poverty consciousness. These things no longer resonated with me.

Their discomfort with the stronger, more authentic 'me' emerging from my tired and sad state continued as I began a new business in real estate investing. Real estate investing grabbed my attention and passion like crazy. I could not get it out of my mind, and even though it was so far from any other business I had created, I was meant to do it. I read and learned nonstop for the next 5 years, becoming very successful and building a large business.

Initially I was so excited about my new passion I would mention it to the women's group. I received some support, but mostly vague and 'oh that's nice' but I noticed no one wanted to really hear about it. Then as my passion grew and I began to really immerse myself in growing that business, I became very focused, motivated and strong, the women became more distant and critical.

"I see myself as wealthy. I believe I AM wealthy."

I began to feel unwelcome in the groups and finally had one woman actually email me a long critical email claiming my priorities had changed, I was no longer committed to the group and its intent and that she thought I should not come to an upcoming retreat. Even though I was aware of the shifts in my energy and attitudes, and that we were no longer on the same page, it was a real blow to me and I was hurt and upset. The other women apologized for her email and so did she. However, it was the point where I realized, I was trying to fit a square peg, me, into a round hole. We no longer met each other's needs. We no longer were passionate about the same things. We were not vibrating in similar frequencies. Bottom line, it no longer worked for any of us.

All along, though, leading up to that, I was feeling inside like I was growing and changing in such a wonderful way. I knew within me I was on the right path for me. There was no doubt. I wanted so much for these women who meant so much to me to honor and respect my new passion. To share my enthusiasm and to support my goals and achievements. I wanted them to become stronger too and more wealth minded, more personally empowered. It was my path, though, not theirs. I was going to seminars that included personal growth and business as well as investing and I was experiencing massive personal growth at levels I had never experienced. When we do this, we cannot expect others to keep up, it has to come from within them. We can never change others, only ourselves.

"My desire for abundance is the Divine source energy moving through me."

I had to stay true to my path and continue, even if it meant the end of my relationship with this group who had meant so much to me. I wanted to stay and yet had to let go and honor my new path. I had to let them be who they were as well. I had spent the previous 10 years or so on a path of intent spiritual growth and learning. Yet, pushing myself in this new area, facing fears of rejection and doing large business deals, and constantly pushing myself outside my comfort zone, was creating spiritual and inner growth on unprecedented levels. It just looked different to these women. Our own personal path and joy has to be our priority. We have to be able to say that we will not let anything stand in our way and we are willing to do what we are drawn to do. trust and let go. As you create a wealthy image, with a wealthy consciousness, you will see who has this and who does not.

"I accept the gift from the Universe to BE personally empowered, joyful, wealthy and happy all the time! I choose this for all others as well. I allow myself to express myself freely and I allow all others the same. I move forward with ease and grace."

Several things happen when you make a decision to change your life for the better. When you begin to take your power and choose what you want, you are going to upset some people. People who know you the way you were, are comfortable knowing what to expect from you and want you to stay that way. It is safe, it is comfortable for them. When you change, the people around you often feel like it is a reflection of their shortcomings. They do not want to change or are not interested in what you are doing. They are afraid you will leave or be better than them. Their insecurities pop up. They often prefer you weak and unhappy, because they can commiserate and relate with you. They are stuck in their own limiting patterns and have not yet discovered their desire to break out of it. When you begin to change, be happy and have success, it makes many people very uncomfortable. Sometimes downright angry and critical. Even if your attitude is not to say anything about it to them, they can see and feel your shifts. Remember, most people fear change.

"I stay true to my vision, myself and my wealth. I let go of the past and embrace the now I am creating."

You have to decide; are you going to be committed to your change or are you going to hold yourself back, limit yourself, and play small to make others feel safe?

Choose people who support your new image

In order to create the life you really want, you have to chose courage, inner commitment and put yourself first. It sounds selfish to our conditioned minds, that have had others telling us since birth that we have to act this way or that in order to fit in and make them feel safe. However, we are not here to live for others, we are here to live a life of exceptional joy and creativity that only each of us has within us. We are here to live wealthy, healthy exciting lives that reflect the uniqueness of who we are and expand our boundaries, and therefore the Universe. It takes a brave heart and a loving soul to venture out past the gates of sameness and Be who we are meant to be. We have to realize, expecting others to be happy and supportive of us, is unrealistic, this is our journey, they have theirs.

Allow yourself and others to BE what you want to Be

Our lives and interests change, and with it the people who best add to our lives. We have times when certain people, groups and careers really excite, push and fulfill us. Then we grow and shift and eventually, we move to something new and those same people, groups and career paths no longer hold the same interest, support and joy. It is OK. It is the way it is meant to be. Let go and move into your next best life and let others do the same. Be careful you do not limit others either. True love, for ourselves and for others begins with allowing. Allow them to be who they are and allow yourself to be who you want to be.

Listen to your inner self

As you create a new, wealthy self image, it is imperative you listen to your inner self. You must choose what is best for you from within, not based on seeking approval from others. Don't wait for outside validation. When you notice someone is negative and it pulls you down, get away and find those who are in your new vibe. We do not have to feel guilty because we are choosing joy, empowerment and happiness. We do not have to justify what we are attracted to and what we want to do and experience. What we do have to do, if we want to live an inner powered life of joy, love and happiness, is be true to ourselves and let others do the same.

Let go of the past

I know, there are people and memories we would love to hold on to. There are passions and agreements that we feel an obligation to stay in. Yet when it begins to limit us, make us unhappy, uneasy and feels as though it is suffocating us... it is time to let go. No agreement is forever, and we have to allow ourselves to move on and to release others, without blame to do the same. What is best for you is not what is best for others and realizing that gives you more clarity in moving forward.

"I absolutely deserve to be wealthy, happy and healthy."

Create your wealth image with very little input from the past. Take only the most positive and empowering memories and extract the feelings and use them. Otherwise, create from the new you. Know that you will need to recognize agreements you made with yourself and others. Then you will need to see if they support and empower your new image. If not, decide to break those agreements in the most generous and loving way possible. It is never about making anyone wrong, not even yourself. It is simply recognizing this is a new you, and part of that new you is one that chooses beliefs, agreements and people that are supportive, positive, empowering. Let the rest go with gratitude.

Choose new agreements with yourself

Many people stay stuck in their old patterns and lives and keep repeating the same negative and unfulfilling experiences, because they are not willing to let go of the old ways and the people who no longer have the same interests. It does not make them wrong, it simply means you have changed and it is time for you to move on and seek new people, places and experiences.

"I think big, I think luxury, I think joy, I deserve. I think outside my box, I open to something new and abundance on all levels!"

Making the transition from where you are to where you want to be involves risk, because you will change who you are with and what you do. You may receive criticism from others and even anger at times from those who want you to stay the same and make them feel ok about who they are. This is not our job. Our job is self care first. No matter what relationship you are in, it does not serve them, us or the greater good for us to deny who we are becoming.

Get support

Most of us need ongoing support as we transform. Having support and being with like minded, uplifting people and information is vital. My coaching, classes and radio show are all designed to keep you supported through all your changes. They will give you powerful tools and techniques to be able to keep strong and positive and forge your path to joy, wealth and love. Having a coach and arming yourself with support is your best way to truly breakout of the same old thing and create an ultimate life. My friends could not see that, they had their own limits in their vision. They felt in sync with me when I was tired and sad. My new found strength and passion made them uncomfortable. Like many people, they had ideas that their way was the best and only way. They thought if you focused on wealth, you were greedy, and were no longer spiritual and had fallen off the path of enlightenment.

Realize that letting go of people opens space for new ones, who will resonate with the new you!

I knew this shift was happening and all along, I was thinking inside "I love these people and I don't want to give them up". I held on as long as I could, even though the energy had shifted for me too and I was no longer feeling welcome, nurtured or stimulated to grow. Their energy had shifted for me too and it all felt very boring, weak and negative. Once the time came I received the email from one lady, I knew inside me I had to leave it behind and move on. My path had diverged and we were no longer vibrating at all the same. I was a bit like a kid inside, throwing a temper tantrum, saying to myself "I don't want to do it". I really did not want to let go of that old security and support, the love and the nurturing.

"I Dare to dream. I know I AM special. I AM wonderful. I AM unique, valued, beautiful and talented! I now align with the Best in everything. I incorporate the BEST of me in all I do."

This is key. When you realize you have changed and others have not, be willing to let go. Not only of others, but of your past or current self that is not aligned with the new image.

Do not continue to hang around people who bring you down, do not feel good, and speak and think in negative or poor ways. You want to make your life exceptional. Find new people who vibrate with the new you and uplift you. Always reach for those who are 'ahead' of you on the curve. Push yourself and don't let anyone hold you back... especially yourself!   Since that group was no longer giving me support or happiness, that was the major clue that it was time to move on and let go.

Choose practical actions that imprint the new wealth image feelings

Create your vision of the wealthy, happy, healthy you. Enhance it by going out and doing things that will give you the feeling of being rich. This is what I call Practicing wealth in my "Wealth Downloads" course. Drive cars, go to restaurants, try on clothes, anything that is what you want to be true for you. This will give you tangible feelings to add to your image and imprint it deeper within you. *"Act as if"*.

Be true to yourself, do not create a new wealth image that is to impress or satisfy anyone else. Find your true self, your passion, your inner light. Once you create a wealthy you, you give others permission to do the same. You model it for them. You can give of yourself, your experience, time, and money and help others. Best of all, your energy goes into the whole and expands the Universe.

A few key things to think about when you create your new wealth image:

- You cannot be a victim and be rich.

- You cannot identify with your lack, your hardship, and be wealthy.

- You have to give up all excuses and take full responsibility for yourself, and your life and everything in it. Period.

- You absolutely deserve to be wealthy, happy and healthy. Own it.

- Think big, think luxury, think joy, think outside your box!

- Dare to dream, know you are special, wonderful, unique, valued, beautiful and talented! Incorporate the BEST of you and everything, and accept nothing less!

I want you to be aware, though, that the image you have of yourself is vital to making any changes in your life. I am designing an entire course on creating your wealth image, your 'Avatar' so to speak. Take the process from the 'Already Rich' chapter and expand on it. Use the key elements here and begin to design the new you from within, imprint it on your mind, and your senses. Watch for it to become! You will begin to tune in to your true wealthy abundant image. Claim it! Enjoy it! Share it!

"I accept nothing less than the Best!"

CHOOSE who you want to BE now. This is all that you need to think about from now on. Let go of the past and move forward, always.

MAGNETIC WEALTH AFFIRMATIONS FOR YOUR WEALTH IMAGE

- I am safe and loved. The Universe is on my side. I have the strength, smarts and courage to handle anything that comes my way. I am supported and follow my inner guidance without hesitation.

- I claim my power. I step into my power. I know my power is Divine, safe and for my highest good.

- I am connected to my true wealth image and the Universe supports me in every moment.

- I allow the unsupportive patterns to dissolve and then take the shape of my new Wealth self image in an instant. I let it go, now.

- I now allow my inner brilliance to shine. I unleash my radiance. I embrace my luster. I am radiant, joyful and prosperous. I love expressing myself fully. This or something better. Thank you Thank you Thank you.

- I now shift my energy to fun and empowering feelings. I choose my life on purpose. I transform through awareness and choice.

- I see myself as wealthy. I believe I AM wealthy.

- My desire for abundance is the Divine source energy moving through me.

- I accept the gift from the Universe to BE personally empowered, joyful, wealthy and happy all the time! I choose this for all others as well. I allow myself to express myself freely and I allow all others the same. I move forward with ease and grace.

- I stay true to my vision, myself and my wealth. I let go of the past and embrace the now I am creating.

- I absolutely deserve to be wealthy, happy and healthy.

- I think big, I think luxury, I think joy, I deserve. I think outside my box, I open to something new and abundance on all levels!

- I dare to dream. I know I AM special. I AM wonderful. I AM unique, valued, beautiful and talented! I now align with the Best in everything. I incorporate the BEST of me in all I do.

- I accept nothing less than the Best!

"WHAT IS YOUR ATTITUDE TOWARDS WEALTH? LOOK WITHIN TO SEE WHAT INVITATION YOU HAVE GIVEN TO WEALTH!"

- NAN AKASHA

LIMITING AND REPLACEMENT BELIEFS

Chapter 14

"Don't ask what the world needs.
Ask what makes you come alive, and go do it.
Because what the world needs is
people who have come alive."
- Howard Thurman

"I don't deserve Money."

"Money is evil."

"Only greedy people who don't care about anyone else want money."

"Money is not important."

"Money can't buy happiness."

"Money or wanting wealth is not spiritual."

"If I get rich my friends or family will not like me anymore."

"I don't want to take away from others."

"There's not enough money."

"Everyone else gets money but me."

We all have versions of these beliefs, installed when we were young. Now we can recognize them and choose new ones. Choosing a new, empowering, magnetic and attractive belief about money is the key. Simply replace the ones that are outdated and don't help you anymore.

I have had many clients who have a disconnect about money. They work hard, are smart, reliable and creative. But often no matter what they do, they cannot get the money to come to them or stay with them. All outward appearances show that they should be successful, and sometimes are, for awhile. However if you hold a belief like the ones I listed above, you have a disconnect.

This means that what you want within you and what you are working towards is not in alignment with what you subconsciously believe. Therefore you cannot receive or keep money. The two realities cannot connect. Your mind will be sure to match your outer reality to your inner image and beliefs.

"Money is my divine right. I am a good, loving, caring person. Money loves me, people love me, and I love me."

We do what I call; follow the thread. You look within and follow what you say you want until you see where the thread is broken. You will run into a belief, a thought pattern or even a cellular imprint that is not congruent with what you now want. You cannot say "I know I am wealthy" and work towards being wealthy, if you have a core inner belief that says something like "I don't deserve money and only greedy, selfish people want money". The inner belief, is part of your Self image. You now know how vital your Self image is in creating change. The inner image and belief will always win. You must replace the belief with one that is powerful in its ability to support, assist and inspire you.

One client had a good job and a successful business. He made good money in large chunks. However, something always happened that took the money away. The car would break down, taxes, business failures.... on and on. He could make the money, he could not keep it long though. Remember, we create our realities. So the place to look is within.

What we discovered was that his mother had always said "rich people are selfish and greedy". He loved his mother. He wanted her to be proud of him. Outwardly he wanted to achieve success and even help her financially, because she was poor (not a shock with that mindset). Inwardly he would not allow himself to do anything that would make his mother not love and approve of him. So if he got rich, his internal belief and image told him, he would be selfish and greedy. His mother would no longer love him. So his mind and wealth image worked together to get rid of the money he made. You will always align with your internal self and wealth image, it is your default.

"Money is good, kind, helpful. Money builds hospitals, finds cures, feeds the hungry and allows progress. Money is love in action. I appreciate money."

Consciously he could not figure out why his money always disappeared and he was frustrated. Once we discovered the disconnect, he was able to create a replacement belief based on what he believed and wanted. The old belief became weak and eventually disabled, and the new one took on strength and created a new wealth image.

Magnetic Process:

Replace your limiting money beliefs with new "Yes" beliefs (Which must be motivating, uplifting and inspiring as well as open you up and energize you! Make it exciting, one that gets your juices flowing). On one side of the paper write all the limiting money beliefs you have. Just keep asking and write whatever comes to you. Then think about your family and any other major relationships you have, who you spend a lot of time with and see if you own any of their beliefs about money, wealth and riches.

Then on the other side, across from each limiting belief write a replacement belief. One that is positive, present tense and empowering. One that counters the limiting one. A true statement of limitless potential. Something short, inspiring, and easy to remember. Something that makes you feel good. Then whenever the limiting one holds you back or comes up, say to yourself "Oh that was the old me, I NO LONGER BELIEVE THAT. I now believe: ____" and state the replacement belief. Do it until it is your default setting.

Here is a powerful statement that is worthy of memorizing and even recording and listening to until you feel and believe it in your core.

Deserving money:

"Money and wealth are my divine right. I am divine. I am a child of light and perfect just the way I am. I am the creator of my reality. The Multi-Verses want me to be rich, happy, healthy loved and joyful. I have an infinite fortune reserved especially for me. I do not have to do or change anything.

Everyone deserves all the Money they desire. I deserve all the Money I desire. There is more than enough for everyone and that includes me. I know what is best for me. I know that my true self is wealthy beyond imagining.

I now claim my right to a never ending, easy to find supply of Money. I am open and receptive to a never ending flow of wealth, money and cash. I know the Multi verses deliver it to me happily, with great love and generosity. I re-claim my natural state of wealth."

So, what is limiting you? Do you know? Can you state at least one thing, right now, that is limiting you and keeping you from the success you crave? Go ahead, write it down.

What most limits us is our beliefs and our conditioning. Our Beliefs are such powerful energy patterns. it is almost like they are a computer chip that, once installed keeps sending out the same signal over and over. It has one message, one that now limits you instead of serves you, which is what it was originally made for. Beliefs are created, and ingrained when we decide something really feels good, or really feels bad. From that, we say to ourselves" Wow, I want that to happen again, a lot, how can I make that true for me?" or something like 'Wow, that hurt, I hated that, I never want to feel like that again! How can I make sure I never feel that way again?".

You may realize that it is not the actual event that is as important, as what we feel and what we decide it means. It is what we choose for the event to mean, to us, that gives it power and juice! Everything that is charged with emotions and deep feeling or conviction, has a lot of power. So things happen to us throughout life, and especially when we are under 10 years old. From those we decide certain things are true for us. Then we forget that that is in our cells and our energy system and it is constantly sending out the same message. Parents are our first hypnotists, followed by the TV. Their beliefs and the way they role modeled Being for us is still within us now. You know, you have them ... it's usually something like "I can't do that" or "I'm not good enough", or self doubting thoughts, anxious feelings that make us feel unsure of ourselves.

"I AM unique, talented, loving, creative and wealthy. I now allow this to show. I now live from the Divine authentic part of me."

So what is limiting you? Do you know? Want to find out?

Magnetic Process:

Choose change. Well, the easiest way to uncover your limiting beliefs is to choose change. Nothing makes your inner dialog (Ego) go crazy like making the effort to change how you think and what you do. You will immediately feel doubt, anxiety, fear, procrastination... You will begin to 'hear' the inner critic, "that won't work", "you'll never be able to do that" and so forth. Write down how you feel and what you think. Be as objective as possible and write down what is going on inside you. When you are able to write how you feel, honestly, do not edit it for political correctness or spiritual enlightenment. We are dealing with what IS, now, accept it.

What did you write? Once you have written out how you feel and all the doubts etc. that are coming up, then wait a few hours or a day and go back and read it. It is a treasure map. It reveals your state of mind, it uncovers a limiting belief, or two. You will be able to see exactly what is going on inside of you. See what you can discover by noticing what words you use, how you say it, and what emotions are coming up.

How does it make you feel? Is it a down energy, one that drains you, makes your stomach turn or feel negative, trapped and less than? If it drags you down and makes you feel less than, it is limiting. If it feels fun, happy, uplifting.... then it is a good belief and you may want to look into it and see how you can enhance it! Now you begin to transform the draining feeling to an empowering feeling. Let the down one go out of your system, and once you feel less emotional, begin to choose the emotions you would like to feel.

Where do you put your energy?

Now you follow your energy and consciously reclaim it. Choose to retract your energy from that belief, those feelings and feed a new one. Conscious energy allotment can really energize you. Choose now to only send energy to things that support and uplift you.

Here is something I use. I use humor with myself, not condemnation. We all have had plenty of criticism, plenty of judgment and plenty of guilt. Now is the time for lightness and love. Don't take everything so seriously. Lighten up, literally, and you will soar. So when I find myself saying anything I realize is negative, self defeating or repellant to money, I say "Oh that's not me, that was the old me, I don't believe that anymore! Now I believe……" and I use a replacement belief or statement of limitless potential. Pretty soon your mind will say, OK, she does not want that anymore and will listen to your new way of being and live from it.

Where are your thoughts?

Where are you looking for help/relief? This is another way to see where your mindset is. Do you automatically begin to blame; yourself or others? Do you complain and make excuses? Counter it in your thinking, "No, that may have been me in the past, not anymore. I now believe _____" Choose a new thought that empowers you and counters the limiting one.

"I AM now irresistible to money. Wealth and profitable surprises are attracted to me in an unending flow."

Make it about you and not about things outside of you. Stay in your sphere of influence...yourself. You made the choices to get here, you can make choices to take you anywhere. Where do you want to go?

Noticing what limits us is like reading a map, a map that shows us where we are going. Is it somewhere you like to go? You must change the inner landscape to change the outer experience.

I hope you enjoyed this one way to uncover and change a limiting belief. Look for my Belief Buster audios!

What we believe about money, wealth, riches, rich people and anything to do with cash has a huge affect on our lives. Because we live in a world that uses money, we have had other people's ideas, emotions and fears about money all around us since birth. Now we know we have taken many of these on, and now it's time to let them go and choose what you want to believe about money.

"I now choose positive, powerful beliefs about money."

Magnetic Process:

Changing how you think and feel about money is vital to creating the life you desire. Here are some questions to ask yourself. Write about them, meditate on them, then use some of the empowering statements of limitless potential below. This is SOOO worth it, when you find peace, ease and joy around the subject of money, your life will flow in miraculous ways!

1. How do you believe money comes to you? (This includes what you think, what you think you have to do, if anything, for money to come to you, and how much you have to do and so on)

2. How do you feel about money? (Are you happy about it? Do you feel comfortable and excited and expectant about money? Do you think it is bad/good? Do you resent or admire wealthy people? Do you feel you deserve money? Do you think if you have it, someone else can't have it and have guilt?)

3. Are you open and receptive for money to come and stay in your life? (If you have negative feelings about this, or doubt it in any way, then the answer is no. If you fear success or failure, or think if you get it you will lose it, this is an important area to address)

"Money comes to me from expected and unexpected sources."

"Imagine a monthly income you can't Outlive"

"Imagine a monthly income you can't outlive..." said a caption in a free magazine...mmmm, yes indeed!

I cut it out and put it on my vision board immediately! What a great idea! I had imagined **"I have more than enough money"**.

I had affirmed **"I am a money magnet"**. I had repeated **"Money comes to me easily and effortlessly from expected and unexpected places"**. I had envisioned an unending , constant flow of money pouring into my life/bank account/business. I have even put up signs in my room similar to; "$30,000 comes to me in June, easily, joyfully, permanently" and put checks written out to me for large amounts on my mirror. It's all awesome. It all works. Do it.

Yet, I never thought to put it quite like this though. I love it. It represents limitlessness. No boundaries, think bigger then big. See broader than ever. Always push yourself to go for what you want. Allow yourself to desire the ultimate. Go for it all. Now, of course.

So let's think of what that means to you. What would an income you can't outlive be like to you? What dollar amount? What lifestyle would that represent to you? What would you do? Who would you be with? It means you can have anything you want, and never worry again, ever. Now.

Could you? Would you? Will you?

Could you never worry? Could you ask for and go for what you truly want deep inside? Ponder it.

MAGNETIC WEALTH AFFIRMATIONS FOR BELIEFS

- Money is my divine right. I am a good, loving, caring person. Money loves me, people move me, and I love me.

- I AM unique, talented, loving, creative and wealthy. I now allow this to show. I now live from the Divine authentic part of me.

- Money is good, kind, helpful. Money builds hospitals, finds cures, feeds the hungry and allows progress. Money is love in action. I appreciate money.

- Money and wealth are my divine right. I am divine. I am a child of light and perfect just the way I am.

- I am the creator of my reality. The Multi-Verses want me to be rich, happy, healthy loved and joyful. I have an infinite fortune reserved especially for me.

- Everyone deserves all the Money they desire. I deserve all the Money I desire. There is more than enough for everyone and that includes me.

- I know what is best for me. I know that my true self is wealthy beyond imagining.

- I now claim my right to a never ending, easy to find supply of Money. I am open and receptive to all the wealth, money and cash. I choose and I know the Multi verses deliver it to me happily, with great love and generosity. I re-claim my natural state of wealth.

- Money is energy, I am energy, I am a natural match to money.

- I am worthy of wealth just by being me.

- All the money I desire comes to me now, easily and effortlessly.

- The Universe is my ally, bringing me all the riches I desire now.

- I have more than enough cash for whatever I want to do.

- I believe that life is to be lived, now, not later. I believe that there is enough of everything for everyone.

- I easily imagine and expect a monthly income I can't outlive.

- I have more than enough money.

- I am a money magnet.

- Money comes to me easily and effortlessly from expected and unexpected places.

"WHEN YOU ARE WILLING TO DO THE WORK, YOU GET THE GOODIES!"

- NAN AKASHA

NAN'S MANIFESTING FORMULA

Chapter 15

What is the most powerful generator in the world?

> *"The acquisition of money is, above all,*
> *a psychological process"*
> *- Richard Paul Evans*

Combine your vision of what you want in your life with the power of emotions and learn to run it through the most powerful generator there is; your heart!

What your heart is really, is powerful electro- magnetic generator. When you know how to use it, nurture it, open and expand it your manifestation speeds up! (I wrote a series of blogs about it this at createyourownrealitynow.com that are very enlightening.) Read them and get started creating in a more natural, easy and effective way than ever before.

Magnetic Process:

Heart Generator; Focus on your heart, open it and see it filing with love and being a huge generator, magnetically attracting what you want into your life. Relax, you are a swirling mass of unending possibilities and the parts of your life that you do not want to live anymore are only one of those possibilities. Choose another one, and step into it.

Manifesting is 3 stages :

1. ASK
2. EXPECT
3. CLAIM

Asking

Asking is asking others, yourself and the Universe or God. You ask on many levels, with words, thoughts, feelings, images and desire. Be sure you are clear on what you want... how can anyone give you what you want if you are not clear about what it is you want. Clarify for yourself what and why. Make it real in your mind with pictures. See the end result, always, in as much detail as you can.

**"I now ask for what I desire with joy, confidence and commitment. I make it real in my mind with all my senses.
I always see the end result in vivid detail. My dreams are real now."**

Wealth mindset tip: ASK. Honor yourself, step into your worthiness and ASK!

What are the benefits of ASKing in a certain way? It is the KEY that unlocks the door to your wealthy, joyous life... truly! There are many ways to ask, with words, actions, body language, to yourself, in your mind, by giving, by doing.

Some things I have received and you will get if you ask:

- I have released my fears around rejection and so I always ask for feedback, and I receive the most amazing, empowering, uplifting and kind comments and testimonials from clients.   Like this "SUPERLATIVE AS ALWAYS!" Joy.

- I have asked the Universe for more speaking engagements, and mentioned it a few times out loud... and the opportunities are showing up like pure magic, seemingly "out of the blue".

- I have released my fear of asking for (and deserving) love, kisses and affection from my beloved. I now receive a flow of them all the time. Now I do not have to ask, because my internal asking and my worthiness are open and receptive and love flows to me!

- I have been asking the Universe for a new mentor and an amazing new one has emerged!

- I always ask for opportunities to increase my business, clients, income and wealth. I have recently received several life changing opportunity that came in a way I would never have been open to before, and yet it appears to be delivering so many things I totally desire! My amazed gratitude for the Universe is so abundant right now!

These are just a few examples to show you how learning to ask is the key to creating your wealth, reality and joy.

Here is a statement of limitless potential for you to use to increase your confidence in asking for what you truly desire;

"I ask for what I want with confidence and ease. I know the Universe is ready and waiting to assist me having what I desire. When I ask, all energy moves into action just for me. I am supported and loved. I honor myself by asking, knowing all possibilities are available for me.

This or something better now manifests for me. Thank you ~ Thank you ~ Thank you"

Expecting

Expecting is the phase between when you have clearly asked for what you want and when it manifests and you receive it and live it. This is a crucial phase because most people fall into doubt here. This cuts the energetic connection. This delays the manifestation. Move yourself into a state of expectation. Believe and trust that what you have asked for is being made just for you. The Universe will never take away from anyone else to give to you, so no guilt, just absolute faith. Get excited. Anticipate it with joy. Plan on it. Prepare and practice. Create space and inner congruency. Be ready.

**"I easily move into a state of expectation. I now believe and trust that what I have asked for is being made just for me.
I am filled with anticipation, joy, and faith.
I am safe and always provided for by a loving Universe."**

Wealth Mindset Tip: Expect Wealth Now

The energy of Expectation is a powerfully pulling energy! Move yourself into the state of expectation to truly get speed into your manifesting. As you move into the vibration of expectation, you are moving into the energies of:

- Trust
- Joy
- Excitement
- Faith
- Belief
- Awareness
- Alignment
- Gratitude
- Celebration
- Active seeking

This state will alleviate your doubts, your anxiety, your worries. It will build your self worth, your 'Wealth Esteem'. You will naturally begin to act in certain ways, because you expect the wealth to come, you will prepare. You will practice, you will look for it to show up!

Expectation is fun! Act like when you were a kid and you were waiting for Christmas or a fair, something you were so excited about you could barely sleep! Expecting your good to show up is energizing, uplifting, enlightening and fun!

If you are experiencing doubts, lack of energy and procrastination, then start to get yourself shifted into expectation. You can only feel those things above, when you are not expecting your good, your wealth, to come to you. If you KNEW it was coming, you BELIEVED it with all your being, you would be happily preparing and dreaming of how great it will be. You will be Grateful for it already! This is real attraction!

"I expect wealth now and always. I am excited as I prepare for my wealth to arrive. I am so thrilled and grateful that wealth is mine and I am ready to claim it!"

Claiming

Claiming is receiving, and they are both an action. Receiving sounds passive, and really, you need to be more powerful about receiving. Claim it! It is a knowing of your worthiness. It is validating. This step, normally called receiving, I call claim. I found that receiving seems too passive and people do not realize receiving is an action. You must be in motion, opening pathways for the Universe to bring you what you asked for. Energy likes movement, money likes speed. As we are expecting it and living in our wealthy state in our mind, we begin to open to receiving. We must claim it when it appears. We must own it. When we do, we enact power and worthiness and it not only becomes our experience but we become it. This is true manifestation.

"I live in a wealthy state of mind. I stand in my worthiness. I open channels for wealth to come to me. I am in motion, aligned with the Universe, co creating joyfully."

"Heart Generator Manifestation" Meditation

How amazing our heart is...it is so much more than anything you could have imagined and so much more powerful than you have given it credit for!

Focusing on your heart opens it, it is a huge generator, magnetically attracting what you want into your life. Here are some excerpts from the special report that goes with the meditation on your heart:

"We take the clarity and vision of our minds and the material of our thoughts, breathe life into it through the powerful electromagnetic transformer within us: our heart. Finally we add the fuel of our intended emotion, the fuel that rockets that creation out of our heart and through our bodies, as the vortex of energetic creation that we are.

...everything is a wave of possibility, of consciousness, of thought. Your power is innate in you. Your power is in your ability to focus and feel. To direct your thought with intention. When you take your focus, add the emotion of Love, you now feel the feeling of what you want. Then your heart, a powerful liquid crystal light transformer, combines your passion and vision, increases the volume and sends out a powerful signal to the world.

Consciously and intentionally expanding your heart, breathing through it and realizing the untapped power in it is key to manifesting the life you want now. Some scientists call it "the 7 layered liquid crystal power generator" We are operating from these scientific truths, using ancient wisdom and knowledge and concentrating on the most direct route to choosing, observing and living the life you desire now.

You will feel your heart change, literally. It will expand energetically, spiritually, it will strengthen physically and it will open, allowing you to feel more pure feelings, and be able to receive and give more genuine love... to yourself and others.

Your heart is your energy vortex generator. Your heart can convert your thoughts, choices, vision, passions into physical reality.

Focus on your heart and feel it's power, feel the energy coursing through it and see it filling and expanding with light.

"The affirmation is empty if it is a thought that has no energy to invite it into this world"
- Gregg Braden

We need to "invite" what we want into this world, this dimension, this vibration. All things are energy that vibrates at different rates. That includes us. Our thoughts are forms, our bodies are conduits of energy , our feelings are our thoughts combined with our emotion. Our feelings give fuel to the affirmation and make it a reality.

"...we are meant to be the masters of the laws of the universe. We are supposed to be in control of the elements, our thoughts, emotions and intentions."

This is how you manifest what you want, but with ease and results, not struggle and disappointment.

Gregg Braden discusses what I call the Heart Generator as *"3 parts of breathing life into your visions of your ideal life"*:

1. **Thoughts**; mind, vision, choice...your specific image of what you want, in any area of your life. It can be your business, your partner, your new dress or your body. You are not your thoughts, however, you think your thoughts, therefore you are in control, in charge of them. So now you can choose a new possibility and "invite" it into your reality.

2. **Emotions**: Gregg says there are only 2 actual emotions (we normally confuse feelings with emotions). Love and whatever you call the opposite of love. Both are equally powerful, 2 sides of a coin and both will pull your vision into manifestation just as quickly. Ever heard "be careful what you wish for"...? There is power in love and power in fear, we are going to now be the director of the emotion we add to our visions, so we get the results (the feelings) we desire.

3. **Heart**: feelings are created in the heart by combining the vision from your thought forms with the power of the emotion of love (choose love). If you choose love, you get feelings like joy, happiness, bliss, excitement, zest, passion, thrill, contentment. This is our ultimate quest. Anything and everything we want is because we think it will make us feel joy and happiness. Feel it now, let your heart broadcast that frequency far and wide.

Focus on your heart, open it and see it filing with love and being a huge generator, magnetically attracting what you want into your life.

"Move forward with confidence, and direction. Follow inspiration, act from excellence, and all things will unfold before you!"

- Nan Akasha

Nan's Manifestation Equation

Ever want answers from life? Me too! Well, I have been receiving some wonderful answers from life lately. Why? Because I am being still and expecting the answers.

I really enjoy meditating, and visualizing and have been in a very intense phase where I spend hours each day in a dreamy state where I see and feel my life the way I am creating it to be. As you probably know, this is the manifestation equation. So here is my simple formula or "Manifestation Equation" for getting answers from life. Be aware, there are some things to do that align you in the best possible way to not only getting answers, but then stepping into the living of your dream.

Begin by relaxing and letting go of all the tension in your bodies; mental, physical and emotional. Drop your awareness down out of your mind and into your heart. Do this till you are truly relaxed and in the moment.

Then make a commitment to yourself to:

1. Let go any thoughts and beliefs that do not support who you truly are in this moment.

2. To be open, willing and receptive to the answers, the guideposts to light your path and to receiving the actual manifestations of your desires.

3. Go deep into the core of who you are, and make your choices from this place. Choose to honor and believe in your VALUE, your WORTH and your right to BE your true self.

Once you are in this space, start the process, take as long as you can, but 5 minutes is enough if you can't spend more time.

1. ASK: Choose what you want, based from your core, and describe as specifically as you can at this time.

2. See (in your mind's eye) what you want, in as great a detail as you can, Build on it each time, adding people, place details, smells, opportunities and more to the vision.

3. Feel (in all your senses as well as in your energy field) how it feels to have, be and do what you are asking for.

Step into the "movie" and make it as real as you can in your body (how it feels to be there, look like that, wear that, how you move, walk, carry yourself)

4. Let the "Holographic Movie" you have created go...watch, enjoy and feel good.

5. Feel happy and grateful for what you are/have and say "thank you, thank you, thank you" as often as you think of it, while truly feeling appreciative.

6. Move into the vibration of expectation. Build the anticipation and faith.

7. See yourself receiving, claiming and living the vision.

8. Infuse yourself with gratitude for ALREADY having, BEing or doing what you have envisioned.

Carry the wonderful feelings with you as long as you can. Repeat to insure you stay in those feelings no matter what you are doing. Carrying the feelings of having, being or doing it with you, brings it into your daily reality more quickly. Being in the state of knowing it is yours and feeling it, will bring you the pleasure now and the actuality sooner.

GO for it!

**"I carry the feelings of my vision with me in each moment.
I look for and find proof my requests are being answered.
I know it is mine. I feel it with all my senses now.
I live in the joyful pleasure of my dream now."**

MAGNETIC WEALTH AFFIRMATIONS FOR MANIFESTING

- I now ask for what I desire with joy, confidence and commitment. I make it real in my mind with all my senses. I always see the end result in vivid detail. My dreams are real now.

- I ask for what I want with confidence and ease. I know the Universe is ready and waiting to assist me having what I desire. When I ask, all energy moves into action just for me. I am supported and loved. I honor myself by asking, knowing all possibilities are available for me.

- This or something better now manifests for me. Thank you ~ Thank you ~ Thank you

- I expect wealth now and always. I am excited as I prepare for my wealth to arrive. I am so thrilled and grateful that wealth is mine and I am ready to claim it!

- I easily move into a state of expectation. I now believe and trust that what I have asked for is being made just for me. I am filled with anticipation, joy, and faith. I am safe and always provided for by a loving Universe.

- I live in a wealthy state of mind. I stand in my worthiness. I open channels for wealth to come to me. I am in motion, aligned with the Universe, co creating joyfully.

- I carry the feelings of my vision with me in each moment. I look for and find proof my requests are being answered. I know it is mine. I feel it with all my senses now. I live in the joyful pleasure of my dream now.

- Money is my divine right. I am a good, loving, caring person. Money loves me, people love me, and I love me

**"YOUR MIND DOES NOT KNOW THE DIFFERENCE BETWEEN YOUR IMAGINATION AND REALITY.
YOUR INNER VISION IS THE TEMPLATE, THE TREASURE MAP TO YOUR IDEAL LIFE."**

- NAN AKASHA

WEALTH VISION

Chapter 16

"You won't get anything unless you have the vision to imagine it"
- John Lennon

"Imagination is more powerful than Knowledge"
- Albert Einstein

Visualization: In my experience, this is the number one favorite technique for manifesting what you want in your life. Visualization is powerful beyond measure. Unless you have experienced the amazing results that ensue when you take time to visualize what you want in your life you have no idea the power of your mind. Visualization has so many benefits that you will be using it and fine tuning it, improving your focus and clarity forever. It is something that is simple and easy and yet powerful and detailed.

"We all possess more power and greater possibilities than we realize, and visualization is one of the greatest of these powers. It brings other possibilities into our observation. When we pause to think for a moment, we realize for a cosmos to exist at all, it

must be the outcome of a cosmic mind"
- Genevieve Behrend

A great manifester and friend said this was his number one technique. He says now that he has done it for awhile, he just sees it (whatever he wants to be, do or have), vividly and then it happens. Every time he thinks of it, he can actually really see it in his mind as already existing. This is key, seeing whatever you want as already done.

"My easiest way to manifest my dream life is by visualizing it. I have visions of what works and then I do it. I visualized a book on prosperity games and then I just did it.
I take action on my visions and then
I have more visions."
- Chris Sherrod, Abundanceunlimited.com

The first way to manifest using visualization is to realize your thoughts are things. You are literally creating mass, with gravity. It is like a holographic image, a virtual reality. Visualization is most powerful when you build your creations in the present, not in the future. Be in the now, create in the now. The now moment is eternal, all that there is really.

Visualization seems like it is future-based, but you are asking for what you want to be true now. If you always see things and ask for things in the future, it is like a carrot on a stick. It will always be in the future. See the end result and pull it into your present.

"I Step into the sensations of wealth, I picture my wealthy life, and my life experience unfolds with perfection!"

Next remember, your mind communicates in pictures, use your vision like a movie and enhance it.

Next build your vision on faith. Decide to have faith in yourself, strengthen your vision and do 5 things every day to move towards your success...then let it unfold before you!

Use symbols and certain visuals to help you get to the vision you desire. Your visualizations may be about letting go, moving on, Being in the new setting. It can be about one thing, or a combined vision of all the elements of your life.

Enhance your vision with sensations, feelings, sounds, smells... Make it as real as anything you have experienced. Then claim it as yours.

"I am fully present in the moment. I drink in all feelings, savor each moment & find hidden treasures all around me!"

Magnetic Process: Rent Your Future

The most power you can give your vision is feeling it as real right now. So much so, you are filled with gratitude for it, just as if it where manifest in physical reality now. We are here to try things out, decide what we like and live it. I find the hardest part for most people is feeling like they have what they want. Most people see only what is already around them, and this keeps them stuck. Here is a way to take the idea of what you want and turn it into a living vision. Your Avatar.

"I have the power to breathe life into my vision. I feel it as real right now."

I always want to find the easiest and most effective way to feel the vision. To train my mind to think always of what I want and how it will feel.

It is like painting a picture and stepping into it.

The idea of "Renting your future" is like going on vacation and renting a car. You order the one you want and pick it up, complete and ready. You get into it and drive off, enjoying yourself. Now imagine doing this with your life. Imagine you are going to rent a body and a house and a pre-formed life. It is a made to order rental place, you fill out the form and submit it. You give all the details of what you want (ever see "Total Recall"? Kind of like that, where he chose an identity and all and they implanted it into him for a "trip" so to speak).

Now imagine arriving and it is all complete for you. Then all you do is step into the 'you' that you ordered and go off, enjoying your life.

So begin by getting your vision clear and placing your order. Actually see yourself on phone placing the order. Then pick up your body and practice stepping in and out of the body, imagining how it will feel. See details, what are you wearing, who are you hanging out with, what are you doing. See from first person (inside you), almost like a virtual game.

"I see myself financially free, in loving relationships, excited about my life and doing what I love."

Do the same with the house you desire or the job or business you want. Feel what it would be like and see yourself actually doing things with the loved ones you seek. Be specific.

Enjoy this like you would a vacation. Do it as often as you like.

More ways to increase the power of your visualization.

1. Watch movies of places you want to be in or go to, people and situations that are what you want, See yourself in it.
2. Make a vision board or vision book. You can cut out pictures from magazines or print form computer. You can write words or cut them or print them out. Divide it into areas of your life like health, wealth, love, and so on. Look at it and meditate.
3. Practice visualizing things you see and enjoy, watch them, seeing all the nuances, then close your eyes and recreate it in your mind.

4. Recreate a fun or empowering event you experienced in your mind. See how detailed you can get and how many sensations you can feel.
5. Go out and DO whatever is a key part of your ideal life to get the feeling, sensations and images.
6. Repeat Daily, or 2x a day.

**"I see and feel my ideal life clearly.
I give great appreciation for
Being Already Rich!"**

MAGNETIC WEALTH AFFIRMATIONS FOR VISUALIZATION

- I am fully present in the moment. I drink in all feelings, savor each moment & find hidden treasures all around me!

- I Step into the sensations of wealth, I picture my wealthy life, and my life experience unfolds with perfection!

- I use my words to change and improve my life. I always speak love, faith, possibility & wealth.

- I see myself financially free, in loving relationships, excited about my life and doing what I love.

- I see everything flowing smoothly, lifting me over the rough spots surrounding me with love.

- I AM ABSOLUTELY CONVINCED that the field of Abundance receives the message of my desires clearly, now and IRRESISTIBLY ATTRACTS INTO MY EXPERIENCE all the good things my heart desires!

- I have the power to breathe life into my vision. I feel it as real right now.

- I see and feel my ideal life clearly. I give great appreciation for Being Already Rich!

"SLOW DOWN. GET OUT OF YOUR BUSY
MIND. FEEL YOUR INNER SELF.
TUNE IN TO YOUR CORE CENTER AND SEE
WHAT YOUR TRUE DESIRES ARE.

THEN CALMLY GO THROUGH YOUR DAY AND
LOOK FOR WHAT YOU HAVE ASKED FOR.
EXPECT TO SEE OPPORTUNITIES...
DOORWAYS ALL AROUND YOU.
FOLLOW THE FEELING OF PEACE, JOY AND
EFFORTLESSNESS."

- NAN AKASHA

How to Inspire Money

Chapter 17

"Follow your bliss and the universe will open doors for you where there used to be walls"
-Joseph Campbell

Do you inspire money? Sound like a strange question? Money is energy just like you. Money is attracted to certain vibrations just like you. Remember you have a relationship with money.

What is your dream? What excites you? What is your "Why"? This needs to be a vibrant, alive thing within you, in order to have the energy, courage, stamina to create the life of your dreams.

I firmly believe... and know, that we each create our own reality. So here are a whole bunch of magnetic wealth affirmations to help you inspire yourself and money! Just think about how you would inspire a person.

"I inspire others to live their dreams. I inspire the Universe to open the doors to my dreams. I allow my dreams to inspire me. I take inspired action now."

MAGNETIC WEALTH AFFIRMATIONS FOR INSPIRATION

- I inspire others to live their dreams. I inspire the Universe to open the doors to my dreams. I allow my dreams to inspire me. I take inspired action now.

- Today is a glorious day for me! It is full of wealth, love, happiness, health and abundance. My heart is filled with faith and resonates throughout me.

- My wealth and happiness is already here. I just continue to connect to it. I trust and choose to begin to see my manifestations everywhere. Thank you!

- I now place all my reliance, faith and trust in the DIVINE power and presence within me.

- I AM wealthy. I feel wealthy. I love being Wealthy. I'm so grateful for my unending flow of wealth!

- Today is the BEST day ever!

- I Claim the riches within me and the riches around me now appear!

- I now CLAIM my riches! It is MINE and it is HERE right NOW!

- Wealth is a joyful state. I now choose to BE joyful and wealth now follows my joy.

- I always believed I am going to live my dreams. I am now ready to live my dreams. I see and feel my dreams unfolding right now. I am living my dreams now.

- I DESERVE. I AM WORTHY. I AM GOOD ENOUGH. I AM AWESOME. I AM AMAZING. I AM INSPIRED. I AM LIVING MY DREAM. I AM fully present in the moment.

- I NOW Re-Awaken to my deepest Dreams.

- I give freely with no expectations. I receive freely with total expectation.

- I release attachments to where, when and how my money comes to me. I am open for money to flow with me, to me from many sources, with joy.

- All possibilities exist right now and I choose to focus on and expect the BEST for me.

- Money is energy. I am energy. I now align my energy to the energy of money and open to the flow with ease.

- I know I am the one that gives meaning to things, and I now choose money to mean joy, health, riches, ease, peace and love!

- My money muse guides me to my riches by nudging me from within. I am aware of this guidance and easily take action.

- Wealth is my natural state. I choose to release all that blocks me from flowing with my natural state and living in wealth.

- I choose happiness. I attract money through my happiness. I am happy, Money is happy. We are a match. We have fun now.

- My Desires Come True Easily...Now.

- My Money muse leads me to the treasure waiting just for me.

- My mind is seeking the path to my abundance on all levels and making me aware of the gateway to it.

- I give great appreciation for my divine ability to Be rich, attract wealth, and to enjoy my unending flow of money.

- I receive freely with no limitations.

- I now willingly, gratefully receive my riches, wealth, financial flow, passive income, cash from any and every direction, easily, joyfully, and I release all obstacles, internal and external, mental, emotional, spiritual, physical.

- I am Open and Receptive to ALL GOOD.

- What I believe is true for me. I decide this moment is the springboard for my greatest good. I embrace my wealth now

I now clearly, unwaveringly, with total expectancy, intend that this is the best year of my life.

In love, In life, In finances,

In joy, In health, in Spirit,

In enlightenment, In expansion, In travel,

In business, In friends, In adventure, In fun,

In wealth, In energy, In delight,

In lavishness, in power, In Inspiration,

In creativity, In speaking, In writing,

In appreciation, In gratitude, In generosity,

In passive income,

In Clear Masterful Communication,

Thank you, Thank you, Thank you.

"LOVE YOUR LIFE...LOVE YOURSELF...LOVE IT ALL...THIS IS THE KEY TO CREATING THE LIFE YOU DESIRE."

- NAN AKASHA

I BELIEVE

Chapter 18

"The strongest single factor in prosperity
consciousness is self-esteem:
believing you can do it,
believing you deserve it,
believing you will get it."
-Jerry Gillies

I believe that you are talented, unique, beautiful, wonderful and loved.

I believe you can achieve, experience, have, BE, and do anything your heart desires!

I believe you are naturally wealthy, healthy and joyful.

I believe you can create any love relationship, friendship, business and income you desire.

I believe if you desire it, it is The Divine expressing through you and it means it is what you are meant to do, and CAN do!

I believe when you play full out, do what you love and trust the Universe is on your side; miracles happen!

I believe you have dreams of stunning, valuable insights that NEED to be shared with the world!

I believe that you are already rich, happy, fulfilled...look for it.

I believe all possibilities exist right now, and you have the ability to tune in to your favorite one!

I believe that everything is opportunity.

I believe when we expect what we want, life unfolds in a never ending flow of goodies!

I believe if you knew that you could not fail, you would release your inner being with release into the world.

I believe when you create and enhance your vision everyday with joy and faith, life is bliss!

I believe that your wealthy, happy healthy self wants to come out to play!

I believe that when you believe this, your life will open up like the clouds parting and the sun shining through onto you!

With love, Nan

"IMAGINE FINDING YOURSELF DRAWING TO YOU, AUTOMATICALLY, ALL THE OPPORTUNITIES, RESOURCES, PEOPLE, RELATIONSHIPS... THAT WILL LEAD YOU TO EMBODY YOUR VISION!"

- NAN AKASHA

WEALTH DOWNLOADS

Chapter 19

"Riches begin with a state of mind, with definiteness of purpose and with little or no hard work."
- Napoleon Hill

Wealth downloads is a ten audio course I created that gives eight new mindsets to install, that attract wealth.

Wealth downloads each contain a necessary mindset that will lead you to wealth consciousness and an open and receptive perspective on life. You will attract, act, and even Be wealth. Listen to each wealth download several times, or until you completely feel you have integrated the concept and are acting on it. The course comes with Statements of limitless Potential (affirmations) that goes with each wealth download to print out and repeat until you have accepted this mindset as real for you.

Freeing your mind requires transforming your old beliefs, perceptions and inner values. These downloads transform your mindset to one of joy, happiness, seeing opportunity, taking inspired action, feeling wealth now, playing with and enjoying wealth and more. Have fun, get rich, enjoy life! I am sharing some of the Magnetic Affirmations from this course with you below.

10 Audios:

1. Introduction to wealth downloads.
2. Wealth Download #1: Everything is an Opportunity.
3. Wealth Download #2: Define Wealth & Indications of Wealth.
4. Wealth Download #3: Practice Wealth.
5. Wealth Download #4: Be Wealth.
6. Wealth Download #5: Let Go.
7. Wealth Download #6: Thank Wealth.
8. Wealth Download #7: Play with Wealth.
9. Wealth Download #8: Open to (receive) Wealth.
10. Wealth Wrap up and 30 day plan.

If you are interested in this audio course, go to http://tinyurl.com/wealthdownloads

MAGNETIC AFFIRMATIONS FROM WEALTH DOWNLOADS

THANK WEALTH

- I AM so joyful and appreciative of Money!
- BEing wealth feels so good.
- I am deeply grateful to Money for blessing me, joining me, loving me, and expanding with me.
- Thank you Money for all the opportunities you create in my life.
- Thank you wealth for enriching my life.
- Thank you cash flow for your consistent and reliable nature.
- I love my abundant finances. Thank you, Thank you, Thank you.

PLAY WITH WEALTH

- I love to play with money!
- I feel playful, happy and excited when I think about wealth and all it does for me.
- I am playing full out and embracing money as my playmate and wealth as my game.
- I AM so joyful and appreciative now that wealth rides to me on the waves of my joy!
- I have fun creating in the field of abundance and attracting wealth while playing my game of life" Thank you Thank you Thank you".

OPEN TO WEALTH (receive)

- I am an excellent receiver!

- I now claim my wealth and rejoice!

- All that is mine by divine right now comes to me and I claim it with great enthusiasm and boundless gratitude!

- I celebrate my infinite wealth now, as I receive it, consistently and continuously.

- I claim my wealth and I am wealth! Thank you Thank you Thank you.

"YOUR JOB IS JUST TO WANT IT, WITH A JOYFUL HEART, ANTICIPATE IT COMING WITH THE ENTHUSIASM OF A CHILD AND RECEIVE IT WITH OPEN ARMS AND BLISSFUL GRATITUDE."

- NAN AKASHA

ABOUT THE AUTHOR

Nan Akasha, CHT

Spiritual Money
Attraction and Wealth
Creation. Magnetic Soul
Alignment and Wealth
Esteem Activator.
Author, international
speaker, Master
certified hypnotherapist, and radio host.

Nan is a contributing author to Joe Vitale's "Expect Miracles" & The 'Vibrant Women's Wisdom' Book.

Nan's many audio products, classes and healing circles focus on transforming your mindset to one of Wealth!

All Nan's work is dedicated to help you connect to your true inner being and power, and unleash a life of joyful wealth in all areas. Trained in over 12 healing modalities, Nan' inspiring, playful, empowering attitude has helped thousands of people worldwide to transform their life. Using experiential learning and powerful tools and processes anyone can repeat.

Nan assists in shifting energy, beliefs and mindsets to release the past, master your Money mind, attune your Wealth vibe and uncover your Wealth Esteem.

Nan's weekly radio show on Law of Attraction Radio Network "Magnetic Wealth" is an experiential show. She takes you on a hypnotic journey and gives you a new Magnetic Wealth Affirmation each week. Nan is the Creator of www.CreateYourOwnRealityNow.com & the amazing "Manifest Your Wealth Now" class. www.MagneticWealthRadio.com

Nan is an expert at going to the core of the issues holding you back in the areas of Money, self worth and attraction energy. Her many original, sourced, empowering audios and tools, are designed to reveal your own personal treasure map to a life of inner peace, joy and limitless wealth.

Living with her beloved Chris, in Austin, Nan is a joyful mother of twin girls, Emily and Sierra. Nan loves life and knows we can all enjoy the abundance that is our natural state.

"EVERYTHING IS OPPORTUNITY."

- NAN AKASHA

Also By Nan Akasha:

- Reboot Your Inner Money Machine Guided Audio
- Manifest Your Wealth Now Audio Course
- Wealth Downloads Audio Course
- The Transform Your Life Series of Audios
- Total Wealth Transformation: Meet Your Money Muse Audio course
- Joyful Creating guided meditation
- Getting Ego on Your Side Audio set
- Awaken to Create Your Day guided daily audio

More: www.CreateYourOwnRealityNow.com

COMING IN 2010

Books:

- "Me First" A guide to valuing yourself & creating the life you desire.
- "Free Your Mind and the Wealth Will Follow"
- "Women's Wealth Esteem"
- Create Your Avatar & your Ideal life. Self and wealth image re creation

Classes and Events:

- Create Your Energetic Blueprint for Wealth
- Women's Wealth Esteem Events
- Magnetic Mindset Series

SPEAKING ENGAGEMENTS

Nan Akasha, CHT is available for live speaking events, online and virtual summits and seminars. Nan has been speaking professionally internationally for over ten years.

Nan speaks on topics from Wealth, consciousness, mindset, beliefs, creating your own reality, healing, energy, Women's esteem and wealth, wealth creation, law of attraction, releasing, stress reduction, motivation, empowerment and much more. Nan is joyful, uplifting, fun, inspirational and transformative. Experiential, powerful, life changing.

To book Nan for speaking, email
Nan@CreateYourOwnRealityNow.com

Nan Akasha's Websites
CreateYourOwnRealityNow.com
MagneticWealthRadio.com
MasterYourMoneyMind.com
Transformationalessences.com
Intendglobalhealing.com
AttractResidualIncome.com
SecretsToMasterYourMoneyMind.com

Nan Akasha's Media Kit Link
Tinyurl.com/nanakasha

CATALOG OF PRODUCTS

BY Nan Akasha, CHT

I invite you to join me on Law of Attraction Radio Network every Tuesday at 8PM Eastern

http://tinyurl.com/magneticradio

Unlock the secrets of your mind and attract wealth and abundance joyfully. Using experiential processes, guided visualizations and journeys, hypnosis and magnetic affirmations we will reveal the riches already waiting for you! Create your ideal self (wealth) image anew, direct your energy, enhance your Wealth vibe and tap into the field of abundance.

As Nan shows you how to mine the riches of your mind, redefine your relationship to money and increase your **Wealth Esteem**, you will begin to see 'Everything is Opportunity'. Call in to work one on one with Nan. Reveal your own personal treasure map to a life of inner peace, joy and limitless wealth. All possibilities exist in this very moment, open to the one that's ideal for you. Join Nan for an hour of wealth, worthiness and fun!

All shows are available on mp3 to download and on Itunes.com. The Magnetic Wealth Radio Show is on Law of Attraction Radio Network.
http://tinyurl.com/magneticradio

Intend Global Healings

What would you like to heal?

"Let go of the past, allow your emotions and body to heal, re-attune to your spirit, align your mind, clear your limiting beliefs...."

Join my FREE healing circle twice a month.

Experience inner alignment... Tune in to a sense of well being and joy.

"I welcome ALL, to put their name into the circle and let go of what no longer serves you.

The earth and all the Universe will join in, not only to be healed, but to be a part of the healing."

- Nan Akasha

IntendGlobalHealing.com

Our combined energies are magic... We can not just move mountains, we can create them, dissolve them... therefore we can do the same with dis-ease, blocks, pain, fear or beliefs.

All past and ongoing shows available on mp3 to download.

TRANSFORM YOUR LIFE CLASSES

Nan Akasha gives frequent Global wide classes available over the web, to transform the key areas of your life. Some of the ones now available on audio are listed below. Please join Nan's newsletter to learn of new classes, events, and specials. You will receive a Wealth Vibe Kit as well, free!

http://www.createyourownrealitynow.com

1. Create Your Energetic Blueprint (for 2010, or anything else)
2. Be An Excellent Receiver; Receiving Wealth
3. The Law of Increase and Wealth
4. Take Control of Your Thoughts
5. Law of Attraction: Lies and Truths
6. Escape the Victim Vibe
7. Release Past & Parents

AUDIO COURSES FROM NAN AKASHA

1. Reboot Your Inner Money Machine
2. Wealth Downloads
3. Total Wealth Transformation
4. Manifest Your Wealth Now
5. Getting Ego on Your Side
6. Joyful Creating
7. The Spirit of Money
8. Awaken to Create Your Day'
9. Create a 30 Day Goal
10. Create Your Ideal Day
11. Intuition Accelerator
12. Yummy Money
13. Unleash Your Limitless Prosperity

All products available at
http://www.createyourownrealitynow.com/

MAGNETIC SOUL READINGS

The purpose of these sessions is to give you direction, clarity, purpose, passion and express yourself. Create the life you were meant to live, and enjoy! Uncover your:
  1. Soul's Type
  2. Soul Mission
  3. Soul Age
  4. Soul's Desire/goal
  5. Soul's Talent(s)
  6. Past life fear operating in life now
http://tinyurl.com/magsoul

MAGNETIC WEALTH ALIGNMENT SESSIONS

45 minute session with Nan to clear and align you with your magnetic wealth vibe! In this process you will experience:
  * Identify your top 3 limiting beliefs
  * Identify your energetic money blocks
  * Identify your repeating money resistant energy patterns
  * Take you through a guided, interactive process to Release, Replace and Activate limiting beliefs, energetic money blocks, patterns
  * Install new mental and energetic process to support your desired Wealth & Money goals
  * Alignment process
  * Give you a personalized Magnetic Wealth Statement to enhance and increase your shifts
http://snipurl.com/magwealth

VIBRANT WOMEN'S WISDOM BOOK

Nan Akasha is a contributing author buy here:
http://tinyurl.com/vibrantwomen

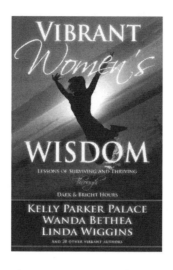

This book will reinforce your belief in the strength of the human spirit. It is a journey through 23 vibrant women's dark & bright hours & their lessons learned. These are brave stories to strengthen & inspire you. You'll be touched by women who overcame, conquered, succeeded, loved, healed, created, beat the odds, lost grew, & shined through! You'll laugh, you'll cry, you'll be inspired.

"This book has the power to encourage and inspire anyone who picks it up. If you are dealing with divorce, abuse, discrimination, medical issues or any other serious challenge, this book will empower you. "
- Bestselling author Caroline Adams Miller

ALREADY RICH! SECRETS TO MASTER YOUR MIND

Thank you so much for purchasing this book. Please purchase some extra copies to share with friends! Give the gift of prosperity!

SecretstoMasterYourMoneyMind.com

CREATE YOUR OWN REALITY NOW

Please join me in creating your own reality! At my site you will find lots of great info, resources, audios, newsletters, classes, free events and more.

Sign up for the newsletter: Spiritual Money Attraction News. Get a FREE Wealth Vibe Kit. I have put together this kit to help you tune your vibration to one that is wealthy, happy, grateful, fun and expectant! Enjoy!

1. Wealth Vibes Audio with Nan Akasha.
2. Wealthy Mindset Tip: Transform Limits
3. Wealth Download #1: Everything is Opportunity.
4. Stress Eraser: dissolves stress.
5. Wealthy Mindset Tip: Anything is Possible.
6. Ask Your Money Muse 2 hour Q & A.
7. The Voice of Debt: transform your perspective on debt forever!
8. Total Wealth Transformation: Meet your money muse audio.
9. Welcome Coupon! I offer you a one time COUPON for 20% off.
10. Wealth Strategy Session.

CreateYourOwnRealityNow.com

Made in the USA
San Bernardino, CA
13 September 2014